HAMMER & NAIL

Caitlin Press Inc.
8100 Alderwood Road, Halfmoon Bay, BC V0N 1Y1
www.caitlin-press.com

Text and cover design by Vici Johnstone
Printed in Canada

Caitlin Press Inc. acknowledges financial support from the Government of Canada and the Canada Council for the Arts, and the Province of British Columbia through the British Columbia Arts Council and the Book Publisher's Tax Credit.

Library and Archives Canada Cataloguing in Publication
Hammer & nail : notes of a journeywoman / Kate Braid.
Hammer and nail
Braid, Kate, author.
Canadiana 20200224247 | ISBN 9781773860336 (softcover)

LCSH: Braid, Kate. | LCSH: Women carpenters—British Columbia—Biography. | LCSH: Women blue collar workers. | LCSH: Sex discrimination against women. | LCGFT: Biographies.

LCC PS8553.R2585 Z46 2020 | DDC 694.092—dc23

HAMMER
& NAIL

Notes of
a Journeywoman

KATE BRAID

CAITLIN PRESS

I respectfully acknowledge living and working at various times on the unceded territories of the Lekwungen, W̱SÁNEĆ, Squamish, Musqueam, Tsleil-Waututh, Burrard Inlet, Tahltan and Taku River Tlingit First Nations. My thanks to them.

This book is for John

Contents

PROLOGUE   9

GETTING THERE   11

FINDING A GATE   12
THIRTEEN STORIES WOMEN TOLD EACH OTHER IN 1960   19
BREASTS? WHAT BREASTS?   20
AND THEN THERE'S FEAR   23
WHEN I WAS A WITCH…   28
…AND A PRINCESS   31
THE NOTEBOOK   33

BEING THERE   35

ON THE TOOLS   36
HOW TO MAKE IT WORK   44
CRANE   59
HOW IT HAPPENED: PART I   61
IN THE BEGINNING WAS THE BODY   73
JOB WELL DONE   80
MAKING MUSIC   90
A NEW DANCE   94
HOW IT HAPPENED: PART II   97
WHICH WAY FROM HERE?   112

FOREVER AFTER

FOREVER AFTER ... 123

WHAT I LEARNED FROM THE MEN ... 124
CONSTRUCTING LANGUAGE ... 130
POSTSCRIPT: WOMEN WHERE? ... 133
MOST RADICAL ... 138

NOTES ... 140
ACKNOWLEDGEMENTS ... 143

PROLOGUE

As I begin to write this, a concrete truck growls outside my window. My neighbour is building a house and today the foundation is being poured. All morning I've opened and closed, opened and closed the window beside my desk. My muscles twitch as if I've had too much caffeine. But it's not caffeine.

I know what the guys on site are feeling right now (and I'm pretty certain they're all guys). They're grateful the rain has stopped, grateful there's a pumper truck nestled in beside the concrete mixer so they don't have to do this job the hard way—filling wheelbarrows one at a time with the gut-heavy mix that is wet concrete. That truck's been here for almost three hours, which means a big pour, lots of concrete, so I also know everyone's tired. But there'll be no rest until this pour is over.

I hear the hum of a pickup truck and guess the concrete finisher has arrived. I leave my desk to peek. Sure enough, a guy in lime-eaten clothes and a handful of finishing tools is walking slowly toward the job as the rest stand back. They're almost finished, feeling good by now—and here I taste a pain as clear and strong as a bitter nut I can bite down on. I close the window. I can't bear to be reminded.

Ten minutes later, nostalgia overwhelms me again and I creep back, open the window just a little to listen....

GETTING THERE

Finding a Gate

So how did a nice girl like me come to yearn for wet concrete like some fading Rose for her young lover? What makes a woman forsake her middle-class upbringing and all cleaner pursuits to embrace mud and sweat? And what does feminism have to do with any of this?

I was born in 1947. As the eldest of six kids, the neighbours called me "the little mother." Family movies from that time show an embarrassingly righteous and self-possessed ten-year-old herding three, four, then five, docile younger siblings. In every photo after the age of six, I'm either hovering over, or have a baby in my arms. My mother was delighted that I wanted to be a missionary.

It was all great leadership training but perhaps also the beginning of my going off the beaten path, because instead of lining up to marry and bear my share of the next generation as Nice Girls were supposed to do, by age twelve I'd decided never to marry or have kids. I figured I'd already raised five, and after watching my parents struggle, and witnessing the impacts of my father's drinking, marriage held no attraction.

I didn't mention this decision out loud. It was simply a fact; I would be a single, childless woman. Full stop.

The only rattle in this otherwise smoothly plotted course was when, around age thirteen, I began a series of battles with my upwardly mobile father that lasted until I was thirty. We fought over everything, though I remember most clearly our regular Sunday night fights over the amount of respect due to working-class people (though I didn't yet use the word "class"). My father was the son of a British ironworker, but as an immigrant to Canada he had worked hard to "raise himself" to an executive position in a national company. Now he mocked everyone—it seemed to me—who carried brown paper lunch bags to the 8:10 a.m. commuter train and returned home (*sans* bag) on the 5:50. In my overly confident junior logic, I couldn't see why these people too, didn't deserve respect. They were working, weren't they?

Eventually, in addition to the people with lunch bags, Dad and I argued about women. It started with comments about my mother—just a farm girl, etc.—until I felt obliged to defend Mum. Then he started criticizing uppity women in general and for no reason I could then articulate, this didn't seem right, either. (Years later, when we'd reconciled, he teased me that I should thank him for the fact that I became both a feminist and a trade union activist, and there's truth in that.)

Those Sunday night arguments were extremely unpleasant, complicated—I realized much later—by the fact they always took place after Dad had been drinking martinis all afternoon. But in hindsight, I could see how they forced me to stand back and see him as a separate person—just another man—so they set an early pattern of not being afraid to argue with authority. Later, in my thirties, when I started to give speeches, sit on committees and engage in arguments with senior men in construction and in government, I dearly valued the advice he gave me the night before my first major speech about women in the trades.

"Never forget," Dad had told me, "no matter what their titles, they're somebody's father, just men, like me."

My mother almost never spoke about my father. If he was late (again) for dinner, or suddenly announced he'd invited eight people for supper the following night, she said not a word. I learned from my mother that a woman bears all and bears it in silence. This was the Golden Rule that good mothers passed on to their daughters in the 1950s, the rule that said it's always the woman who gives. Who else could it be?

I accepted the Rule—it was what my mother and her women friends lived by—because I had nothing with which to oppose it. Yet I could not abide by it. It affirmed what I later read by poet Louise Bogan who in the 1920s wrote that, "Women have no wilderness in them, / They are provident instead, / Content in the tight hot cell of their hearts, To eat dusty bread….They wait, when they should turn to journeys."

I was clear I would not live my life eating dusty bread, but to say to my mother, "I refuse to be your kind of wife," was beyond imagination, disloyal. The only option I could see—and this seemed daring enough—was not to be a wife at all.

❧

I was the first person in our family to go to university, and it was a Saturday afternoon in the summer of 1966 after third-year university, when my life turned. I was sitting in the cool of our rec room reading a thick, blue paperback called *The Feminine Mystique*. The house was uncharacteristically quiet, or maybe just every other sound had faded behind my focus on what I was reading. The drapes were closed to keep out Montreal's heat and humidity, and in the dim, cool interior I was only partway through the book when I stopped reading and laid it carefully, face-down on the couch beside me.

I felt as if I'd been driving down the same road for years and suddenly noticed a major street I'd never noticed before. How had I missed such an inviting, open, obvious avenue? Betty Friedan, the author of this small bombshell, had just thrown open the lid on a modern Pandora's Box. It threw light on all the questions, the hunches and crazy urges I'd had for years but for which I'd had no name. Until now I did: feminism.

You'd think everything would have been clear after that, but I spent the next forty-five years, and continue still, integrating the implications of that book into my life.

❧

In those days, girls had three choices for work: you could be a nurse, a secretary or a teacher. Very recently there was a fourth choice as stewardess on one of the new commercial airlines but for that, you had to be a registered nurse. Since I couldn't stand the sight of blood, and didn't want to teach, I chose secretary, by default. Even now, it's surprising to remember how shocking—how exciting—it was in the '50s and early '60s to imagine supporting myself, earning my own money.

At university I took a BA with Secretarial Certificate—"something useful" people said—and my first job was as a "temp" in London where I'd been travelling but had run out of money. I was hired to help the president's secretary in a large British company. At school I'd been a hotshot at taking shorthand but not so good at reading it back, so when I took my first dictation, I returned the so-called "finished" letter directly to the boss with a polite note asking him to please fill in the blanks where I couldn't read my own writing. At the time I thought it a rather clever solution, but the man's permanent secretary did not. She took me behind a door to politely, firmly, suggest I move on.

On the second temp job, I erased a bank president's signature while using an ancient copying machine—really, they should have replaced it years ago—and realized that perhaps secretarial work wasn't for me. But if not secretary, then what? I dabbled at this and that—public relations writing, child care, teaching ESL, receptionist, going back to university even, thinking perhaps I'd teach?

It was the mid-'70s and women were waking up, asking questions. By now I was living in Vancouver and I began going to Consciousness-Raising (CR) groups—discussion groups for women where anything and everything could be brought up, talked about, questioned. It was exhilarating and terrifying, but mostly exhilarating.

The CR groups were my guide. Until now I had accepted the common saying that women talk too much, that our eagerness to talk was a weakness. Now, slowly, I was coming to see that it was—it is—in fact, our strength. With few exceptions, the world we were living in was built neither for us nor by us, nor was it being recorded by us or for us. To my surprise, I was discovering that women's lives were not even mapped—at least, not by women. I had to ask other women, over and over: *How is it for you? Honestly?* And they told me.

It was happening across the country, across the continent. In Vancouver, women formed a Caucus and started a women's newspaper, the *Pedestal*, that the rest of us poured over, uncovering new injustices.

And injustice was everywhere, much of it focused around the issue of lower pay for the same work as men. The right to birth control and abortion were also becoming issues that could actually be talked about in public, though I never heard the word "sexual harassment" until a conference organized by the BC Federation of Labour in 1982. Women formed a Women's Health Collective to educate us all about our own bodies and I spent one afternoon sitting on the floor in a circle with a half-dozen other women, our legs spread wide, inspecting our vaginas with flashlight and speculum. Red and lush and moist—they were beautiful! Why had we been ashamed?

There were petitions and parades and International Women's Day on March 8 became a major event, with rallies and workshops and classes. It was all incredibly exciting and yes, a liberation, though we later realized, it was more a liberation for the white, straight women like me, than for many others. The rare woman who mentioned the rights of lesbians, or women of colour, was a surprising and usually lone voice. At the time, dazzled by our own courage, we straight white women couldn't see how other women's rights could possibly differ from our own. It was a failure of our time, one that marked a liberation still to come.

But in spite of the excitement and changes feminism promised, as I neared the age of thirty, I was in near-despair. I felt lost in a no man's land of Non-Identity: I was Not Married, Not Mother, Not Nurse, Not Secretary, Not Teacher—not to mention I was Broke. I was almost thirty years old and still didn't know what I wanted to "be" when I grew up. What was I going to do with my life?

I'd started back to school, taking a master's degree, thinking maybe I'd become an academic and teach after all, but by 1976 I couldn't handle the questions anymore. I needed time to think. I dropped out of university for what I thought would be two months, to live in an isolated cabin on the Gulf Islands off the coast of Vancouver. It was there I wandered into construction.

Two months on the island turned into six, then twelve, and I was almost out of money, no matter how frugally I managed. I'd looked for local jobs as waitress, babysitter, clerk—but there was nothing. Then, at a party one night, a friend suggested I apply for his job as a carpenter, building the local community school. He'd just quit. It came out as easily as if he was taking off his shirt on a sunny day. It was ridiculous, of course. In 1977, no one had ever heard of a woman in construction. But desperation was about to uproot the mighty oak of tradition. What else was there?

I owned a pair of steel-toed boots from working the summer before piling lumber in northern BC, and the guys lent me a tool-belt and a hammer. After a quick lesson from the men ("Lie," they said) and a sleepless night spent dreaming up "credentials," (maybe I'd sort-of-built a house up north?) I applied the next morning at the foreman's hut, shaking with fear—and by some miracle, was hired as a labourer. Later I'd find out the guys had been slowing down on the job and he'd figured that maybe having a woman around would get them to speed up, show off. He never expected me to actually do anything.

I never in my wildest dreams ever imagined being a carpenter. Why would I? Everyone knew girls can't do construction. In high school, we were forbidden to take shop (and boys weren't allowed into Home Economics). I never hung out with my dad in the garage. We didn't have a garage. And if anything went wrong mechanically in our house, Dad would order Mum to "Call the Man," as if some generic trades god could/would/did, fix all.

But within a week on that first job, in spite of (or because of?) fatigue and blisters and aching muscles, I loved construction with the passion of a drowning person who has bumped into a boat full of friends, food and wine. Still, it would be another two years as a labourer plus a four-month pre-apprentice course before I dared to say, "I want to work as a carpenter." I couldn't even imagine, *being* a carpenter, let alone a skilled journeywoman. Simply being able to swing a hammer, to build a house, seemed wildly ambitious enough. It had taken a while and the way hadn't been exactly clear, but with some luck I'd found an opening, a gate to what looked like an interesting future.

It was one of the unthinkable desires that, years before, Betty Friedan had given me permission to think, and now to act on.

THIRTEEN STORIES
WOMEN TOLD EACH OTHER IN 1960

1. Stay in the circle. There are many rewards.
2. Don't excel. This is not one of the rewards you were promised.
3. Let the other one go first. Always. Say you don't mind.
4. Don't make noise. Quiet as a mouse, like a mouse. Don't call attention to yourself. Remember that!
5. Look after the others (first). Somebody has to do it. Why shouldn't it be you?
6. Don't be greedy.
7. You can win a prize for improvement but never for being the best.
8. You're only as good as the person you're helping.
9. Good women help others (preferably men) excel. Good women do not embarrass everyone by themselves excelling.
10. If you look after others, you will have no time for your own goals. If you win, you are not looking after others.
11. Winning calls attention to yourself. Shame on you.
12. If the above are difficult, you can always fall back on shame. Shame is the punishment for not staying inside the circle.
13. The circle is the circle of being a glorious victim. Don't try and start new circles. It's not allowed. They said so.

BREASTS? WHAT BREASTS?

I always took my breasts for granted. In a family of four girls and two boys, I was too busy being the eldest to pay much attention to my body, and by the time I began to enjoy sex, breasts were just another part of the picture—not the main actors, but playing a lovely supporting role.

So I took breasts for granted—until I started construction.

On that first day when I applied for a job as a carpenter, my hands were shaking. And my breasts felt suddenly huge. People with breasts do not—cannot—do construction. Even today, most people think that's true, and in 1977, everyone did. So after breakfast I changed my clothes, then again, until the offending breasts were disguised—I hoped—by the loosest T-shirt I owned, covered by a baggy, over-sized man's shirt.

It seemed to work. The foreman acted as if this was normal, as if (fe)male persons regularly dropped by his shack to ask for a job—though I found out later, none ever had. I was hired for $6.50 an hour, more money than I'd ever made in my life at traditional "women's" jobs. He hired me not as a carpenter, thank goodness, but as a labourer, someone who does what they're told, carrying ("packing" the men called it) endless piles of lumber, plywood and nails to wherever they were wanted on site—and in the process, learning the names of tools and work procedures and how to look like a real construction worker.

Except for the breasts. No one else had them, and I continued to wear the Double Shirt Shield until one day when temperatures had been running above 90°F all week. For almost a month the guys had been working shirtless, and Jim, our foreman, was getting boring with his line of, "When will you take off *your* shirt, Kate?" He and I had been working together all week, roofing, bent over black asphalt tiles that sucked up the heat and reflected it back onto our sweating faces, our backs splayed to the sun. We were building a school and the roof we had to cover seemed endless. So one morning in desperation I threw my highest coverage sun-top into the backpack along with my lunch.

The moment came at around two that afternoon; I couldn't stand it anymore. While everyone else was busy nailing, I climbed downstairs, found a quiet space and changed into the sun top, then climbed back up, put my tool belt on and knelt to begin hammering as if nothing had changed.

But it had; I was naked. Or at least, I felt naked. The guys seemed to feel it too because surely it wasn't just my imagination that suddenly the usual banter had stopped dead and the roof was very, very quiet.

"Talk it up, boys!" Jim suddenly ordered in his gruffest, I-am-the-Boss voice. "Talk it up!" and the banter started again.

Still, I was grateful when the weather cooled, and I could go back to my two-shirt uniform.

Three years later I was working on a crew, framing a three-storey walk-up apartment building in the West End of Vancouver. By this time I had some confidence as well as some skills. I was a third-year apprentice who'd been to school enough to know something about framing. Besides, the best framer on the job had taken me under his wing and was teaching me the tricks of the trade so I was almost beginning to look like I knew what I was doing.

I liked working here. It was the first job I was ever on where we actually talked—the guys and I—about more than cars or sports. We even got as personal as food. There were no pin-ups, and I had a fair share in whatever swearing went on. I liked the work and we were all united in our firm dislike for the company's owner who—luckily—rarely showed up and then only to give a few token orders, tell us we were doing it all wrong, and disappear again. So, when the owner wasn't there, I'd started to relax a little, to notice, for example, that when I walked across the deck on a newly laid floor with tools hanging familiar at my sides from my tool belt, if I exaggerated the swing of my hips the littlest bit, I could create a small music of pry bar, hammer and square. It was fun. I'd even got so bold as to take off the outer shirt and instead wear a coverall over my T-shirt—double protection, and cooler.

But it got hotter, and one day, in a to-hell-with-it moment, I went to work wearing the coverall and under it, only a sleeveless undershirt. I was "out" now—this apprentice had breasts. I knew they might even be seen bulging from the sides of my coverall.

And a strange thing happened. We all now knew The Girl had breasts and sure enough, the men began to treat me differently—almost (was this possible?) with a tiny bit more respect. One guy offered to get me more studs but since that was clearly my job, I said no thanks and got them myself, but I appreciated the offer. There was suddenly the tiniest sense of gentleness in the way they talked to me.

It was as if it was all right—finally—to be a woman on a construction site, a woman with breasts. As if confessing—"Look guys, I'm female!"—was a coming-out. And breasts were OK.

AND THEN THERE'S FEAR

I'd worked as a labourer and apprentice carpenter building houses for four years, but this was my first union job. Only unionized companies do high-rise towers like this one, and I'd always wanted to work with concrete. All morning Lorne, my partner, and I had struggled to finish forming up the concrete tube that would become an elevator shaft for this downtown high-rise. Our workspace was small and jammed with lumber, screw jacks and formwork as we placed a series of six-by-six reinforcing posts, bracing for when the next floor was poured. But to set them on the inside, it was becoming clear someone was going to have to hang over the shaft.

Lorne was six-foot-four and weighed at least 200 pounds. Besides, after a few weeks of working together we both knew that hanging anywhere, sixty feet above the ground, was not Lorne's thing. That made it the apprentice's thing. I was the apprentice.

Lorne grunted, "Better get yourself a safety harness."

I'd never worn a safety harness.

When I checked the tool room, all the safety belts were huge, made for big men, so the foreman sent one of the labourers out to buy a belt that would fit me. When he came back, he handed it to me with a bit of a smirk—or was that a dare? It was a thick woven-fibre thing, and Lorne showed me how to step into it like a cloth seat. I settled myself and tied the buckle tight. He snapped its metal ring securely to a piece of steel above, and with only a small shiver of anxiety, I pushed out.

When I got over the breathless feeling, it was like being on a swing—sort of—but with a very different view: straight down sixty feet to a steel grey bottom and up to a blue sky, all with the damp, half-water, half-earth smell of fresh concrete. Lorne growled something about, "We're not here to sightsee," and I got to work.

Still, I treasured the feeling of (mostly) exhilaration, the breathlessness of space, of knowing that what I was doing had to be done, the next necessary step in building. I also knew I was gaining a few more points in the men's eyes, though that was a minor thing at the time. Hanging in the shaft of a high-rise, there's a fierceness of concentration, an *I'm alive!* feeling that pops champagne bubbles up and down your veins—like rock-climbing, but getting paid for it. I had discovered the crushed-ice taste of fear and exhilaration and physical strength, and when I swung back to the solid concrete of the deck, I was changed. Now I understood the puffed-out chest, the swagger of macho. I had danced the fine footwork of danger, pushed past fear and survived so that now I too was entitled to boast. This is why carpenters and mountaineers and farmers walk with a certain confidence. We push to our physical limits and survive. The clearest description I've read of this mix of excitement and danger came from writer Diane Ackerman who, when asked if she was afraid or if she felt daring when learning to fly, said, "I don't feel particularly daring. For me…it's just a case of my curiosity leading with its chin."

ℳ

During the fifteen years I worked in construction, women occasionally asked, "Weren't you afraid?" It was never another tradeswoman—they already knew. It was women who'd never dreamed of physical labour, who believed the line about, "Women can't do this work." But was I afraid, working on high-rises and bridges, hanging off the edge of buildings, walking along three-and-a-half-inch top plates when putting on rafters?

Not really. Cautious, definitely, and careful of the everyday, obvious dangers. Everyone's taught in trade school how to work safely with saws and knives and chisels, how to be aware of heights and keep a workplace safe. Mostly, I did all that. The odd time I didn't—a single step backward into thin air, working two storeys up and not bothering with the safety harness—those things didn't happen often, and never more than once.

No, the real fear hit when I walked into the carpenters' shack on a new job and first met the men I'd be working with, or rather, when those men realized they were going to be working with me. For virtually all of them, I was the first woman they'd ever worked with on the tools, and after a few jobs I knew how it would go.

When I opened that door, there'd be a sudden group intake of breath, a freeze frame of motion, until one brave soul ventured something like, "Oh, a girl on the crew." If I was lucky, it was said in a neutral tone. Then movement would resume—and was I just imagining it or was everyone somehow more careful, quieter, as I hung my tool belt on an empty nail and someone pointed out a space where I could leave my tool box? Then it was my turn to take a deep breath and find an empty place at the scarred plywood table. I'd open my Thermos and, trying not to tremble, pour a cup of tea, just like the others, like the men. But not, because I was The Girl.

Everyone's nervous on the first day; I knew this after I'd been on crews for a while and watched other new guys arrive. They were thinking: How will this new crew be? Will the foreman be fair? Will he care about safety? But after a day or two they'd settle in and then—unless he was a man of colour, or Indigenous, or gay, or in some other way an exception to the Straight White Man paradigm for Canadian construction workers (still)—he wouldn't worry about it anymore. At least, that's how it looked.

For me, it was ongoing. This was the 1970s and '80s. Even today, women are rare on construction sites except as flaggers. But eventually, I got it. These guys had been coming to this same-old-same-old workplace for the past thirty—heck, for the past 1,000 years—and suddenly someone with breasts is sitting in *their* place at *their* table. What went on in their minds when they saw me? A flash of surprise, shock, that frozen silence, were the only clues I got. Most of them covered it well. I had to be watching their eyes when I walked in or I would have missed it entirely. Occasionally, someone would actually welcome me, or say it was good to have a woman on the job, but that was only on Day One.

Construction guys covered most things well—except when they feared or even hated me. "Nothing personal," as one guy said, "just that you're a woman." I was grateful. At least he'd said out loud what I'd suspected, even called me "woman" instead of "girl." But nothing personal?

How personal is gender?

At first, I thought I could deal with it by looking and acting like a guy. If being a woman was a problem, then no problem—I'd be one of them. I wore baggy clothes, stopped talking, made notes. It took more than three years of trying harder than I've ever tried anything in my life, to realize I couldn't do this, couldn't be a guy.

℀

Every day I had to be guarded, prepared for how any particular man might react. He might be fine one day, then have a fight with The Wife the night before and decide to take it out on me. Or one who's watched me carefully for a few days, even a few weeks, is suddenly alarmed at how capable I am, especially after I'd spent ten and more years in the trade. What if women can have babies, do the emotional housework at home and *also* build—do "men's work," as people tend to call it? Suddenly that guy decides I shouldn't be here. If he's my labourer, he starts ignoring me, not bringing the materials I need so the foreman gets mad at me, wondering why I'm suddenly so damned slow. Or he's my partner, and suddenly stops telling me what the foreman just asked both of us to do, so I can't foresee what's coming.

My first line of response was always to be nice. Then I'd try teasing, sweet-talking and impressing them. I made jokes, I ignored them. When none of that worked with one particularly obnoxious guy, I yelled, "Fuck off!" into his face and after that we were best buddies. He told me later he'd just wanted to know where I stood.

Perhaps it wasn't exactly fear I felt at work, but a constant state of watchfulness. From time to time, on the worst jobs, people would ask why I didn't quit—was I crazy? And yes, sometimes it felt that way. If I loved the work and was good at it, wasn't that all that mattered? Why was this so complicated? It didn't hurt that I'm stubborn and didn't want to walk away from the best money I'd made in my life. So every morning for fifteen years, not counting weekends and lay-offs, I picked up my tool belt and my pack with its Thermos of milky tea, sandwiches, cookies and an apple, put on my steel-toed boots, took a deep breath, and went to work.

WHEN I WAS A WITCH...

In 1978 as I was starting my pre-apprentice course, I met a man, John, who had me seriously reconsidering my early vow never to marry. Luckily, there was that sort-of acceptable option of "living together." And that wasn't exactly marriage, was it? So we moved in together, and John's seven-year-old son, Kevin, moved in with us.

But in 1984 we split up—permanently, I then thought, though Kevin still spent one night a week at my place—and I was shaken. I'd been working as an apprentice and journey carpenter for several years, both union and non-union. In that time I'd also worked with two other women carpenters, Chryse, then Jacqueline, doing small renovation jobs. But I'd never met another woman on a large construction job. So somehow I was back to that old question: Who am I now? As a construction worker I felt powerful, yet also terribly vulnerable. As a woman, I felt mostly a failure. Men looked at me as Weird, women looked at me as Superwoman, and somehow the confirmation of the few other women carpenters I'd met didn't seem to count. So which was it, anyway: Powerful or failure? Weird or Superwoman?

Perhaps it was trying to find an answer to that question that sent me to a Hallowe'en party that year dressed as a witch.

My roommate spent all day getting me ready. She covered my face with white pancake makeup that had a faint bluish tinge, and painted my lips deep red. I'd washed my hair the day before and left it twisted into dozens of tiny plaits that I undid just before the party so it sprang up in tight dark curls all over my head and across my eyes. Then I put on a long, stylish black gown I'd bought, cheap, at the Sally Ann. Finally, I picked up the old broomstick I'd painted white the day before, and I was ready.

At the party, I danced with complete concentration only on my broomstick, ignoring anyone who watched. Fuck 'em, I thought. I'm a witch. I have myself and my broomstick. I felt like the lone woman that night who didn't look at men, didn't see them, didn't need them. I had secrets I wasn't tempted to tell. This was in the days before lesbians and trans people could be open about their sexuality, so people stood back, watching.

The women were curious but let me be. The men hated it. They tried to joke with me, to take my broomstick away, move in to dance with me. When I shrugged them off and ignored them, they got angry, raised their voices. "What's with you, anyway?" I kept dancing. When I turned away for a moment, one of them stole my broomstick and hid it. But instead of being pissed off, I was amused. By that time I felt just fine, dancing alone. I'd already learned a precious lesson—that the power of the thing is in the withholding. These men felt they must be wanted, *must* be paid attention to. I held a power in myself I'd never dreamed.

The next year for the Hallowe'en party, I changed personas. If men were going to be afraid of the solitary woman, then I'd come closer, share their walk, their clothes, look them straight in the eye, join them in the male clubhouse. That year I disguised myself not at all and went as I dressed every day of my working life—as a construction worker. I wore my usual hardhat and blue jeans, beat-up steel-toed boots and my pink plaid mackinaw shirt with a pack of cigarettes tucked into the top pocket for effect—their brand name, "More," a conspicuous invitation. Instead of a broom, I slung my sledgehammer casually over one shoulder.

After a few years in construction, I knew how men walk, how they talk. When I got to the party I swaggered, bumped into people—men, women—just a little. Got out of no one's way. Never apologized. I raised my eyebrows at men and women both, but with different messages in my eyes: to the men I said, "I know you." To the women, "Hey, sister!"

The men didn't know what to do with me. They got giggly, looked around as if caught. I walked their walk, seemed to know their secrets. They tried to ignore me, turned away, then back—how could they ignore one of their own? She's a—what is she, anyway? One of us? She must be one of us, she knows the moves. A nudge of my elbow, tightening of the jaw, a nod. Get it?

It was the women who surprised me. They fell over themselves, titillated, excited, like birds. Like girls, they sought to come under my pink mackinaw, and it wasn't just the women who I knew were lesbians that reacted this way. Was it always like this or was it just that year that all the women dressed as stereotypes? They were prostitutes and dance hall girls, except for the few who were exact opposites— frowsy housewives dressed in the haute couture of thrift stores. I narrowed my eyes at them and they nearly swooned. One tried to steal my cigarettes, so I grabbed them back, maybe just a little roughly. She loved it.

The men tried not to watch. They didn't have to—they knew this game of tease-and-hustle. It was when they all moved away and the women moved in that I made my own move—and left.

It was the last Hallowe'en party I ever went to. None of us were really masked at all. We had stamped large on our hungry faces exactly what we wanted, who we already were, or thought we were, or thought we were supposed to be. This wasn't play at all, it was a dead serious search.

I'd tried the two extremes and neither fit. As I stepped down the front stairs to go home, I was thinking I'd have to find another way of being. I felt good in my self, in my body, in my work. I didn't care anymore what anyone thought. It was time to give up costumes.

...And a Princess

When I was a girl, my favourite fairy tale was the one of the Beauty so passive she was asleep. Her prince was handsome, of course, with pitch black hair that matched her own and he fought valiantly, including through a garden of thorns, to get to her side. In some stories he fought dragons, but I preferred the one about thorns. Everyone knows there are no dragons.

I was an intelligent child. I knew the story wasn't true. It only had to be perfect. So when I grew up I planned to build the castle of my dreams. I would build the tower surrounded by the messy garden where my prince would know where to find me. But first I ran into the problem of boots.

As a modern princess I needed steel-toed boots for building. "Sorry, m'am," they said. "We don't make women's boots. I don't care how many of you there are, we don't make 'em. We don't wanna bother. But if you insist, what size do you take in men's?"

When I took my training as a building princess, my muscles grew large. I rejoiced at carrying materials with names that rippled off my tongue like exotic fruit—"joist" and "purlin" and "beam." I lived up to my dreams.

When I moved into my castle, my voice got lower and stronger. I learned how swearing helps and I used it as my sword. "Get off our god-damned backs, boss man," I said, and his hair rippled in the wind of my breath.

The first prince I ever met said, "Lay 'er down. Lay 'er off." I left.

When I told the second prince that I was making more money than he was, he said it was unladylike, and left.

The third likewise said I was not a good princess. "You stomp the rocks with your boots and dare to ask what I'm doing on your property," he said, "just because I act as if it's my own. I'm leaving!" And he did.

I am a damned good princess and I have discovered others the same. We grip our hammers tightly, these tools that built our palace walls, the walls that keep us warm. We planted those thorns for a purpose. All princes may apply at the gate.

The Notebook

It started on the island, on that very first day I worked as a labourer in construction. Apart from being utterly exhausted and having blisters on my hand from hammering all afternoon, I was confused. I'd liked the guys—I think. But most of what they talked about made no sense to me. Mostly they didn't talk at all, not like any women I knew. Instead, they grunted. Their conversations—if you could call them that—were one-liners or, even better, one word. And yes, they joked a lot with each other, but I usually didn't get the joke until a few minutes too late. And then there was the vocabulary: joist, shiplap, crescent wrench. It was all so weird!

I was living alone at the time. So after supper and a nap and having no one to talk to except my cat and my dog, I jotted down a few notes about the day. Maybe it would help me understand what had just gone on?

Over time, it became a habit. Every night after work I wrote down the things I'd liked at work that day, the things I hadn't, what the men had said, those jokes. It calmed me somehow, made it all seem just a little more comprehensible, as if I was ever-so-slightly more in control of what was going on.

After a while as I got busier at work, the notes got shorter and shorter until one night, I thought some of them looked almost like poetry. Was it possible? I'd imagined becoming a poet even less than I'd imagined becoming a carpenter. But by then the writing had become a habit, a part of every workday and eventually, I would take a writing course, join a writing group and start writing poetry and prose in earnest.

BEING THERE

On the Tools

Early morning. I'm living in a neighbourhood where there's construction going on, and as I pull my chair up to the desk, a circular saw roars into action outside my window. I have an idea for an essay and am wondering how to start it when the saw calls again. "Talk about me!" it screams. "Talk about me!" So—as a warm-up exercise, just for fun—I do.

Construction workers carelessly refer to any electric saw as a Skil saw, but Skil is a brand name, like Kleenex. Technically, it's called a "circular saw" for obvious reasons; it's one of the only tools in the shed that's round. Maybe that's why it has to so fiercely guard its reputation as the most macho tool of all.

When you work with this saw daily, when it's the first tool you pick up in the morning and the last you put away at night—carefully—then the circular saw takes on a personality. No kidding; this one throws its weight around, talks loud, bites fast and hard if you don't treat it with a little respect. By which I mean, a *lot* of respect. This one figures it's a heavy dude and some of the best-known American versions—Skil, Milwaukee, DeWalt, Black and Decker—hold solidly to the rule of, "Might makes right." One website calls this saw, "The great American power tool." Of course.

Myself, I prefer the Japanese-made circular saw: Makita. It's a samurai that stands out for its rich turquoise colour. American-made saws—screaming red and yellow—hoot, *Wooser! Girly colour!* but my little Makita holds her ground, has her own deep dignity. It's true she's smaller than the others, and lighter, with a smaller handle so that small hands, Asian, or female perhaps, can get a firmer grip and hold her for hours with less danger. But most important, she's reliable.

Everything about her is beautifully engineered from the starting trigger to the handle and the depth adjustment that raises and lowers the plate.

And tough? Maybe because she's built for work and not for show, the everyday quiet quality of this tool will outlast any of those chest-puffing American Just-Watch-Me daddys. Makita doesn't waste energy strutting her stuff with noise and dust. She just quietly sets to work. One Samurai pass of the blade and you're done. Next!

Did I say the circular saw was invented by a woman?

One day I was feeling cocky in the lunch shack and asked the air, "How come every tool we use is longer than it is wide?" I knew it would make the guys nervous, but I wanted to shake them up a little and see where the dust settled. There was an anxious flutter, then the shop steward said, "The circular saw isn't longer than it is wide." There was silence while we all considered this wonder, then a deep voice said, "The circular saw was invented by a woman."

That took the stuffing right out of me.

"How do you know that?"

He wasn't sure, he'd heard it somewhere, but I went home and did the research. Maybe it's wishful thinking but there's a time, a place, a name. The name is Sarah Babbitt, a Shaker woman who in the late 1800s was watching her husband and another man cut one of the huge first-growth logs that no longer stand on the American East Coast. (And while we're at it, not many on the West Coast, either.) At the time, the technique was to lay the log over a dug pit. One man got into the pit, the other stayed on top and they applied a six-foot-long saw blade with deep rakers (the teeth that clean sawdust out of the cut) and plenty of muscle to slowly slice slabs off the tree.

Watching the enormous amount of energy this took, Sarah noticed their saw cut only on the push, so that half of all the cutters' energy was lost. She went into her house, cut a metal pie plate into small sharp teeth, slipped it over the hub of her spinning wheel, fed a cedar shake into it—and the circular saw was born.

⁄⁄

The saw outside my window is quiet now, perhaps in a moment of awe in honour of its lineage. But it sets me to thinking of other tools I relied on when I worked as a carpenter: sliding square, level, nail puller, and of course, the hammer.

I can hardly bear to speak of my hammer, almost sacred. Don't laugh. Would you laugh at your fingers? Your heart? A carpenter's hammer is like that—an extension of her flesh, warm wood and cold metal that work with her no matter what the weather or how she feels—though in construction, feelings are far, far down the list of priorities.

(Tell a foreman you're not feeling well today and you'll get a guffaw and a finger pointed over his shoulder. "If you want sick," he might say, "how'd you like a trip back home for the day? No pay?")

No, carpenters don't feel; we work. And if you don't like something, just hit it harder, with your hammer—a sledgehammer, if the 22-ouncer in your hand isn't heavy enough.

Am I sounding macho? Hammers can do that to a person. With your hammer—your own hammer, never anybody else's—you're ready. With a hammer you can do anything.

Nobody lends their hammer. I learned this when I worked on the Metrotown SkyTrain station in Vancouver. I was a journeywoman by then, just off a six-month stretch of working with another woman carpenter on our own jobs, and now I was back with the union, with the men. One thing I always loved about union work was the size of what we built: high-rises, bridges, SkyTrain stations. I also loved the pay. What I wasn't so fond of was the attitude of some of the guys. About my hammer, for instance.

On the first day at Metrotown I was sent to start the footing forms this station would stand on.

"I'll send your partner along later," the foreman said.

Ten minutes later as I was hammering together an awkward little brace, sitting back for a second to think about my next step, a large hairy hand pulled the hammer from my hand.

What, the…?

A small man with a head of curly black hair was beaming benevolently down.

"You hold the hammer like this," he said, giving a totally unnecessary demonstration.

Usually in these situations I am patient, polite. But this guy had caught me unawares. Without thinking I stood up and grabbed my hammer back out of his hand.

"I know exactly how to handle a hammer," I said with clenched jaw, staring hard and slightly down into his eyes. It's convenient I was taller than he. "And if you ever try that fucking stunt again," I said calmly, "you'll find out precisely how well I handle it."

I can be a real construction worker when I have to.

Speechless, the man stepped back and stared at the ground for a moment. Good.

Then he said, "I'm Mario, your new partner. What are we working at here?"

Very good. I gave him the instructions the foreman had given me earlier and the two of us got down to work. After that, Mario was an angel to work with.

Construction workers like it big. In their toolboxes at home most handy people probably pack a 12-, at most a 16-ounce hammer. On the construction site, especially a framing job where it's all hammer, most of us carried a 22-ouncer. And every week I went for a massage of my right forearm where the therapist squeezed out searingly painful knots of muscle and tendon and sent me home to ice them so I could work again, swinging that hammer without pain, for another week.

One Monday a few minutes before work started at 7 a.m. we were all sitting, bleary-eyed, around the plywood table in the carpenter's shack, Thermoses open and coffee steaming, most of us wishing we were still in bed, when the door slammed open and Marty, one of the carpenters, burst in. He could hardly wait to tell us the news.

"Eat your hearts out, fellahs!" he announced. (I was considered an honourable fellah by then.) "Wait 'til you see this baby!" And out of his backpack he whipped a huge, I mean sledge-sized hammer that he waved aloft as proudly as if it was an Olympic banner.

"Isn't she a beaut—32 ounces of pure power! And look at the length of that handle!"

There was a moment of stunned silence. I could smell the envy. If they'd called themselves pagan, if they'd dared, most of the men in that shack would have been down on their knees, hardly daring to raise their eyes to such power. For me, the association of length of handle to heaviness of head was more than glaring.

As if to rub it in, Marty grabbed the nearest hammer out of someone's tool belt and held it up to his giant. Sure enough, it was Popeye and Peewee, Zeus and a withered elf. Even I, The Girl, was in awe. And I couldn't imagine what shape Marty's arm was going to be in after a whole week, let alone two or three months of work with that monster.

That's how construction workers dealt with male sexuality; we flaunted it. We did it bigger, harder, longer, without ever saying the "P" word. Which is why I was happy to carry a 22-ounce hammer, and to use the smaller Makita saw. Yup, I had to admit I was a Girl, but Endurance—that was my specialty.

Of course, the way to endurance, to working this hard, day after day after month after year, was our tools. We kept saw blades and chisels sharp and immediately replaced anything that broke, though they rarely did because we usually bought the best we could afford. Tools were so key to what we did that that's how we spoke of our work. "When I was still on the tools..." a construction worker will say, usually nostalgically.

※

And then there were the basics—like the steel-toed boots.

Thirty years later I still have those boots; I can't bear to throw them out. They're a dashing shade of deep burgundy with beige trim, tied four inches above my ankle. After a few years they were so worn, the toes so scuffed that you could see the glint of steel toe under the leather. The guys didn't know I cared about the colour and I wouldn't have dared to tell them.

It's one of the things I learned in the trade; you don't confess to strong feelings, unless maybe it's for a car, or a hockey team. You never talk about family, don't breathe a word about the kids. Still, to myself I could confess: I loved my boots, even if they were a man's size and I had to wear thick socks.

Those boots were one of the few reliables on every job; they protected me. The soles were a solid half inch of Vibram with a tread I couldn't wear off no matter how much concrete or plywood or wet mud I scuffed across, no matter how steep the roofs I walked. Metal insoles kept nails out. Thick brown laces that put dints in my fingers when I pulled them tight, kept my boots on, held me up, wouldn't let me slip. In those boots I was safe.

℀

Then there was my tool belt. Think of your little sister, think of the necklace your mother left you when she died, think of the Bible with four generations of family Births and Deaths written inside the front cover in your grandmother's hand—that's how personal, how familiar, how precious my tool belt felt.

It didn't look like much: beige leather. I bought it at Rona, or maybe at Standard Lumber. In fifteen years, I only had two belts. I'm thinking of the second one now. It had a large pocket on each side that perfectly opened to my closed hand—the hand that entered empty and came away full of spikes or two-and-a-quarter-inch common nails, or with a saw wrench or chalk line, plumb bob or.... Those big pockets were like the trunks people relied on when they went for long ocean voyages. My pockets held anything, everything I needed. I loved their softness (pale suede, not hard leather like almost everyone else's). I loved the depth of the pockets, the darkness of them. My hands could hide there. *Did* hide, though you wouldn't be caught dead with your hands in your pockets when a foreman came around. No, you'd pretend to be looking for something, even if it was time, a moment's pause in a hard-working day. This was another thing I learned from the men.

In front of each big pocket was a smaller one. These were like the hand luggage where I kept small nails, screws, whatever I needed for that exact job, that day. The little pockets gaped a bit but that was fine. If I was using handful after handful, I needed the small pockets to be open, available, fast.

To the outside of each small pocket was a series of leather slits where I kept the smallest things: pencils, an awl, the odd screwdriver, nail sets. Even on the roughest jobs, you could always use a nail set for a spike that wouldn't sink home. And below those, again on each side, a loop.

Boy, those loops! That's where the hammer went. Some guys wanted metal ones that would clank and rattle when they walked—macho, noisy loops. Not me. I loved my soft suede ones, silent, beautiful loops just there to do their job—like me. What I wanted was not the sound but the *feeling* of my hammer swaying—the weight of it at my right hip, easy to my right hand. I wanted the slight pull of it. You know that feeling when you're about to get your period and there's a downward tugging at your core? That's how a hammer feels. Its weight says, "I'm here. Just a reminder. In case—whenever—you need me." And it swings. Carrying my hammer on my right side, with the nail puller and sliding square in the loop on my left, was like walking with a grass skirt over naked hips. Sensory? Hell, it was sexy.

On the good days.

On the good days, which came after about three years in the trade, on a crew where the guys had decided I was OK, on the good days I'd swing across a newly laid ply floor with the smell of sweet-cut fir and hemlock rising like the steam of a spa around me, sun shining down like a thousand warm candles, and flaunt my way to the next spot I had to work.

I thought only I knew how sexy it was until one day, on a framing job, one of the guys invited me to go with a few of them for a beer after work and I said—suddenly afraid—"Where are you going?"

"Why?"

"Because I don't want to go to a place where they have exotic dancers."

And he said, "I hate to tell you, Kate, but every time you walk across that deck, it's an exotic dance." And that's when I knew how good I was feeling on that job because I actually laughed. I wasn't uptight or worried about what he was thinking of me or afraid there'd be some repercussion later, a threat. I just enjoyed it, taking it the way he meant it, which was pure admiration. I flaunted it when I walked and he'd seen and it was OK. That's something else I learned from the men in construction—that men can just watch. And that the fact they're watching doesn't mean they have to participate. As women, we'd want to get involved. Not guys. They're so into their eyes, most of them can be happy to just look. Really!

⅞

There were lots of fine men in construction, men who watched me for a few days or a few weeks, then offered their help. This was the best—when a carpenter took me under his wing and taught me what he knew. It's how men have learned their trade for a thousand years; you have to do it, and you have to be shown by the ones who know, who've done it themselves for years. I have university degrees as well as a carpenter's ticket so I know theory and certainly, there's lots of theory in the trades, especially if you want to build stairs or rafters. But it doesn't do much good to know the theory of a hammer or a nail or how to walk the narrow top plates of a wall; you have to know how to swing that hammer and hit each nail, how to balance, all day, every day, for years. This is physical learning, in the body—our primary tool—and it's one of the things many of us most love about our work.

⅞

Outside my window, the saw is singing again but this time it's sharper, cleaner. Someone has just changed his—her?—saw blade and the instrument is quieter now, doing more easily what it does so well—making progress, making shelter for people. Just doing its job, building.

How to Make It Work

In trade schools, we women are taught the same skills as men, but nothing is said about the trades culture—that unique blend of dress, language, ways of acting and values that over the years have become "the way to be" on a North American construction site. So even today, it's depressingly common that after a year or two, a lot of women get tired of being "the foreigner" and drop out, retreat to some other job that's perhaps less satisfying but where they feel more welcome, or at least more comfortable, as women.

I figured this out—and stayed on the job for several more years—after I read Deborah Tannen's book, *You Just Don't Understand: Women and Men in Conversation*. The book was written in 1990 and has some of the limits of its time in not considering the impact of some of the broader aspects of diversity such as race, ethnicity and sexual preference, but in its focus on gender, it provided me with an invaluable second look at my place as a woman in an overwhelmingly white, male, heterosexual workplace.

Tannen is one of several American linguists who have researched the differences in men's and women's speaking styles, and how that's reflected in our behaviour. She says most North American men engage in the world, "as an individual in a hierarchical social order" in which they're either one-up or one-down. Conversations are "negotiations" in which it's important to keep the upper hand and not feel pushed around. Life is "a contest, a struggle to preserve independence and avoid failure."

On the other hand, she and other linguists have found that most North American women engage in the world "as an individual in a network of connections." For most of us, conversations are "negotiations for closeness" in which everyone tries to reach consensus. Life "is a community, a struggle to preserve intimacy and avoid isolation." So while most men operate in hierarchies of power and achievement, women's communities are more of friendship. Relationships for most women are therefore held together by talk, but relationships for men are held together by activity—a ball game, a few rounds of golf—rather than talking about that activity. Which is probably why sports is one of the main topics of conversation around the lunch table.

Of course, these are generalizations and there are lots of exceptions, but I found this enormously helpful in understanding what at first had seemed utterly peculiar to me about the way men relate at work.

What if we could offer women who are new to construction a guidebook, a sort of "Ms. Manners for the Non-Traditional"?

Keeping in mind that this is by necessity a general picture with lots of generalizations and a few exaggerations, such a book might read like this:

1. The Mega-Muscled, the Mighty and the Rest of Us: Strength

The most common excuse for not hiring women for blue collar, physical work used to be, "They aren't strong enough." (Though note some of the heavy furniture female cleaners routinely have to push around.) This excuse is heard less often now, partly because it's against the law to refuse someone a job based on their gender, but also because so many women are actually doing the work.

In two trips across Canada, from Yukon to Nova Scotia during which I interviewed women miners, carpenters, electricians, welders, boilermakers, machinists, heavy equipment and crane operators, labourers and others, I didn't meet a single woman who'd had a physical problem she couldn't handle. It's just that most of us handle the physical challenges *differently* from men.

Kinesiology experts say if you take averages, then the "average" man is stronger than the "average" woman. But strength varies so much between individuals that the generalization is almost useless. An inch of muscle is an inch of muscle, the experts say, so some women are stronger than some men because they have more muscle.

The difference that makes a difference is in quantity, but also in the *location* of the muscle. Men's strength (muscle) tends to be concentrated in their upper bodies—shoulders, arms and back—while women's tends to be greatest in our lower bodies—hips and legs. Watch how most women carry babies, perched on their hip, while most men carry a child in their arms, using upper body strength. One of the advantages of women's strength being where it is, is that our centre of gravity is lower, which may contribute to better balance. For other reasons, mostly to do with more body fat, women also tend to have better endurance to cold and heat.

So if you're a small woman, or out of shape, don't be discouraged. There are ways to make up for lack of strength, including spending time in the gym, building strength and endurance over time on the job, and learning techniques and "tricks of the trade" like balance and leverage. Sliding a length of pipe over the handle of your wrench for more leverage, for example, will give you the strength of two.

Your male partner will probably use upper body strength to throw that 80-pound sack of cement or asphalt roofing tile over his shoulder. You'll probably find it easier to use your lower body strength, hugging the load close and carrying it on your hips. We've carried babies like this for centuries. Note that for some men, carrying a load "differently" counts as not carrying the load at all. Don't be intimidated. All the foreman cares about is that the material gets from A to B as fast as possible.

But there's another complication; as women we assume, often as the first woman, that we must work hard to please the boss. (And sometimes we're overtly told this.) We know we're being watched as a representative of our entire sex and if we don't do well, it might be a long time before they hire another woman. (Often, we're told this, too.) So we work very hard to prove ourselves. But the harder we work, the more we're in danger of rousing the men's resentment for "showing them up."

If you really do need help on a job, ask for it, or find another way to do it using leverage, the crane, whatever—that doesn't hurt you. And if all else fails, ask for help! Two people carrying drywall up a staircase can do more than twice the work of two people working separately, with less strain, and less damage to banged-up walls and stairs.

By the way, if you handle the job safely, it's amazing how you'll notice men later (quietly) doing the same. A shipyard welder told me that after she started on the job, a foreman told her the men had started asking for more help—and things got safer for everyone.

In fact, it's a hidden "strength" of women that if muscle doesn't immediately work, we tend to quickly consider alternatives. "Use your brain, not your back," tradeswomen tell each other.

A male firefighter gave me an example of this when he told me about a fire in which a man went down (collapsed) while fighting a fire. When two male firefighters couldn't lift him, a third—a woman—seeing brute strength hadn't worked, noticed he was hooked on a piece of metal. She pulled him loose, then carried him to safety, not over her shoulder but dragging him, using the strength of her legs and hips.

But strength isn't everything. Apart from getting the job done quickly, the other thing every foreman is watching for is attitude. Ask any boss; someone who's committed, reliable and hard working—even if they need training—is a more desirable worker than one who might be stronger or even more skilled but who has a big chip on his shoulder, or who regularly shows up late or hungover.

2. Health and Safety

Any good job with more than a few carpenters will include a Health and Safety Committee, with someone—usually one of the crew or the First Aid Attendant—as the Health & Safety Officer. If you have any concerns about health and safety on your job—as many construction workers did, for example, during the coronavirus pandemic—talk to your Health & Safety Officer. Most Worker's Compensation Boards (WorkSafe BC in British Columbia), have a 24-hour telephone line open seven days a week. Here you can ask questions or report serious incidents, fatalities or unsafe work conditions. Check their website and keep their toll-free number handy—in Canada 1.888.621.7233 (1.888.621.SAFE). Remember too, that you have the right, by law, to refuse to do dangerous work. If you think that what you or a colleague are doing puts you at undue risk, report it to your supervisor. If the supervisor refuses to take action, contact WorkSafe yourself. This can be done anonymously.

Every job has its dangers but the dangers in construction tend to be conspicuous, often involving blood, broken limbs and even death. So be vigilant. Every time you use a power saw in one hand, check to see where all five fingers are on the other hand. *Every* time.

3. The Clothes

As the only woman, you're instantly conspicuous. Spend a few weeks, or however long it takes, getting comfortable on the job before you decide whether or not to express your individuality with spray paint and sparkles. Some men will assume you're just there looking for sexual partners. If you wear heavy makeup and no bra, they'll be certain of it, and make your life a lot harder. Then they'll say you asked for it.

Dress practically. You can buy cheap work clothes—T-shirts, shirts, jeans, coveralls—at second-hand stores. In the men's section the clothes will be looser, better made and cheaper. Wear layers. Almost anything you see in men's work wear stores will be lighter, warmer, won't bind your movements and, when the weather changes, can more quickly be pulled on and off than anything from a women's store. (Remember: in construction, time is almost everything.)

4. The Food

The good news is that you're now going to be burning a lot of calories so you never have to worry about going to the gym. Eat healthy to keep your energy up. I always packed the biggest lunch on the crew, also usually the only one with fruit in it. On a large job there may be a coffee truck that comes around at breaks to sell sandwiches, drinks and chocolate bars, but the time you spend waiting in line is time off your ten-minute break. (Did I mention that when the boss says, "Ten minutes," he doesn't mean eleven? What are you doing still sitting there?)

At first, you may find you're more thirsty than hungry. Drink plenty of fluids; you'll be sweating. There's some controversy about salt tablets but I found that a mixture of juice and mineral water was best at replacing the sugars and salts lost in sweat. Legally, water must be provided on the job for drinking but it's rarely (except perhaps in times of pandemic) available for washing.

5. The Talk

The first time you hear lunchtime conversation on a construction job is usually the first time you'll know for sure you're in a foreign country, only this one sells no postcards. Remember, a construction worker's talk is usually based on hierarchy, on who can be the best, funniest and quickest in repartee. Guys love to put each other down—in fun. Well, sort of "fun." If they do this with you, and you notice they've been doing it to each other, it's probably meant to include you and make you feel like one of the crew. Take it as a compliment and try to quip back.

This was such a new skill to a lot of us in Vancouver Women in Trades that at one of our conferences, we sponsored a whole workshop on Witty Comebacks. On jobs where I needed them, I carried a few of my favourites on a scrap of paper in my pocket. Practise your one-liners, and use them the next time the slightest opportunity comes up. The guys will love it. Now you're learning the lingo! In the competitive culture of the trades, you've just "one-upped" somebody.

Most guys love to laugh at anyone who's been one-upped—even better if it's in public with other guys around to see it.

If you're not good at one-liners, or stuck for a come-back, just smile. It's amazing how much you can get away with, and what you can say, if you smile while you're doing it. (It was another journey-woman, Marcia Braundy, who gave me that useful tip.)

Another aspect of construction workers' talk is the swearing. Although many men *don't* swear (and won't like it when or if you do), it's not uncommon in trades work. Sometimes, when a woman comes on the job, men will stop swearing because there's a Lady present—especially if they see themselves as Gentlemen off the job. It's meant to be respectful, but if it keeps up, they'll resent you for "making them" stop swearing. If you start swearing to make them feel more relaxed, they resent you because, "Ladies shouldn't swear."

This is a contradiction where you're damned if you do and damned if you don't and there's no way out as long as the men think (and you expect) they should treat you like a lady. You're a trades-person now, making as much money and expected to do the same work as the men, and it's important you let them know that though you might need the usual help given to apprentices or anyone new on the job, you don't need extra consideration. So if someone says something about a lady on this job, you might want to remind them there are "Only tradespeople here." This is not to deny you're a woman, only to show you don't need special treatment. Trust me, they'll be (secretly) relieved.

Remember that the men on your job are probably also strug-gling with this new situation. Most men who've never worked with a woman in construction (which is most men) always thought this was "men's work," so what does it say about them when a woman arrives on the job? So, as with language, a man who sees himself as a gentleman may feel obliged to offer to help "the little lady" carry her materials. If she allows this, she's resented, by him and by any others who notice, especially the foreman. She's being paid the same as him, so why should he do her work and his too? But here's the bind: if the woman says, "No, thank you," and insists on doing her own work, a man feeling obliged to act as a gentleman may feel that she's trying to show him up. It's another no-win situation.

So be assertive. When a man offers help, assume he's just trying to be helpful. Smile and say, "Thanks. I appreciate the offer, but I can do it myself." This is valuable information for him (and all the other guys who will instantly hear about it). It's important they know you *want* to do your share of the work, even if you have to struggle a bit at first. This earns big points in respect—though of course, they'd never say it.

6. "Feminine" and "Masculine"

Traditionally in North America, especially before the second wave of feminism in the '70s and '80s, a desirable woman was defined as, "feminine," that is, physically weak, mechanically ignorant and (preferably) beautiful. "Beautiful" meant thin-bodied and big-breasted as revealed by short skirts, low necklines and high heels. Helplessness was a plus.

Women who work in a trade become physically strong, mechanically competent, assertive and—to work safely—wear loose shirts, blue jeans, hard hats and steel-toed boots. If there's something we don't like, we speak up—definitely no softies. Does this make us less feminine?

Which also means that a lot of the men we're working with who call themselves masculine because they do dirty, physically difficult "men's work," may find themselves shaken. What does the presence of a woman make them as men?

Men and women working together for the first time in construction are building new definitions of "masculine" and "feminine," as men and women in offices have been doing for years. Hopefully, if we can all be respectful, this process will be a smoother one.

7. Just Testing

When you start a new job, especially if you're a rookie, you'll be tested. Everyone in construction gets tested. It's nothing personal, as the men say, just a way of seeing how you fit into the hierarchy, how good a sport you are, how good your skills (because skills are instantly obvious, noted—and respected). So if someone asks you for a yard of shoreline or a skyhook, joke along. Even better, ask them first. Now you're starting to fit in!

Sometimes women are deliberately asked to handle heavy weights, just to test us. Know your limits and make your own decision as to how far you're willing to push them. They'll respect you for this, too.

Sometimes, while "just testing," men will push a bit too hard, get a bit nasty. Take every assertiveness course you can and don't get angry, don't get scared—this is all part of the culture. Just smile (remember that technique?) and push right back. Stand your ground, say what you think and if you possibly can, say it with humour. Nine times out of ten that guy will turn out to be your best friend, saying lightly, "Just testing." A guy likes to know where you stand.

The tenth time may be a case of genuine harassment, but you won't know that until you've tried the assertiveness test on him first. Never assume harassment.

8. But Yes, There Is Harassment

As one male construction worker succinctly put it, "When you walk onto the construction site, you're the new kid on the block and it's your turn to take it. Get over it." That's testing. But there's a difference between this and what comes from the few really bad apples, the bullies on the job. This is harassment, and men—not just women—have stories to prove it, of co-workers and bosses who didn't want them there, who determined to get rid of them in any way they could, not excluding violence. Men who get this extreme treatment don't like it any more than women do, but they'll do their best to hide it. As one male heavy equipment operator told me, "A guy might be going through hell on the inside, but he'll say nothing on the outside."

It took me years to realize that if someone on the job is being harassed, everyone knows it but almost no one ever does anything about it. In any situation—not just on construction sites—it takes courage to speak up when someone else is being unfairly treated. In the trades, women call it the "pack mentality" and define it as men's unwillingness to break that unspoken male bond that never criticizes another man's behaviour.

The best explanation I heard for this was from a high school shop teacher.

When I asked him why men say nothing when they see a woman (or a racialized person, or a small guy, or a gay guy, or anyone else who's a bit different) being harassed, he said, "Because the men don't want to insult you. If they stepped in, it would imply you couldn't look after yourself. That would be condescending." This was shocking to me—not at all what I'd been thinking!

Whatever the reason, if you've tried assertiveness and the guy hasn't backed off, then it's time to up the ante. Go beyond assertive; get aggressive. Saying, "Fuck off, asshole!" two inches from someone's face can be successful. If you can do it with a smile, he'll be so confused, he probably won't even get mad.

A good foreman should have an eye out for this on the job, and if you're lucky, will look after the problem—either talking to the bully or, if necessary, laying the trouble-maker off.

But if that doesn't happen, don't be afraid to ask for help: talk to your union job steward, the Health & Safety Rep or to a friend on the job who might be willing to speak to the problem guy, or at least, give you some tips on how you might deal with him. Remember, if someone is being a jerk, he's not just a jerk to you, he's a jerk to everyone. He may be picking on you because you're a woman, on someone else because they're Muslim, on a third guy because he's short. But the problem is him, not you! Never fall into thinking of yourself as a victim.

9. The Porn

Pin-ups can be an emotional issue for men and some take them very, very personally. One researcher has called them "totems," evoking "a kind of worship," which in my experience doesn't overstate it. So just asking a man to get rid of them often doesn't work, may even guarantee more porn the next day. For this reason, most trades-women I know try to just ignore them. We sit with our backs to them, eat in a different lunch shack, go out of our way to avoid them.

Or you could try guerrilla tactics. One woman countered the female pin-ups by putting up male ones, and suddenly all the pin-ups came down—male as well as female. Another woman who had no success with that tactic, and who knew most of the men on her job were devout Catholics, put up a postcard of the Virgin Mary. By noon the walls of that shack were virgin pure. Get creative!

I never did understand why some men were attached to porn. One man explained to me he had a right to "beauty" in his life. I offered him a poster of flowers in place of the porn but no, it was only the pin-up he wanted. Another explained it a little differently. "In the hard, dirty world of construction," he said, "a woman's body represents one of the few soft, really beautiful things I know."

A third man, uncomfortable with a co-worker's pin-up, persuaded him to take it down by telling him, "If I put up a picture of a guy with a 12-inch, steel-hard penis, you'd feel bad. That's how a woman feels when she sees your poster with its 44-inch bust." Most women would find this reasoning ludicrous, but in this case, it worked; another example of some of the deep differences in our two cultures.

10. Our Own Gender

It's clear that some men feel uneasy or even threatened by women who step outside traditional "feminine" boundaries and they'll look for ways to tag you: girlfriend? mother?... Sometimes one of those tags is that you must be a lesbian—especially if you've just rejected his sexual advances. He (and sometimes women, too) may be assuming lesbians "just want to be men," doing hard physical labour.

Don't be intimidated and don't let your own fears of their assumptions separate you from women who might be valuable allies
on the job regardless of their (or your) sexual preference. The real
message behind the, "You must be a lesbian," tag is that you're rock-
ing the boat. They'll just have to get used to it.

11. In Praise of Work: Taking It Personally

Every tradesperson makes mistakes on a regular basis. Stay alert and
catch them before they're permanent and have to be torn out. Learn
from them. As one of my bosses said, "Everyone makes mistakes. It's
how you fix them that matters." Another was famous for saying, "If
you can't hide it, highlight it!" Mistakes make you a better tradesperson. You may not be perfect, but it's OK to be merely excellent.

If anyone notices you're having trouble—with a nail, say—tell
them (as a guy would), "There's a heavy wind blowing!" And he'll
laugh. Remember that the focus in trades work is on getting the
job done as fast (and incidentally, as well) as possible. Any seeming-
ly harsh personal comments made in the process are not intended
personally—contradictory as that sounds to most women's ears. The
boss isn't yelling at you, he's yelling at what you *did*. It took me years
to learn the difference. Over and over, women hear, "Don't take it
so personally!" Yet that's a thing that, in our upbringing as women,
most of us have been specifically encouraged to do—to be concerned about how others feel, to empathize, take everything personally. But in a trades culture you get no points for "sensitive." Don't
look for approval or back-patting. Assume that if nobody's yelling at
you, you're doing a good job.

This can come in useful in other parts of your life, too. I learned
from construction to be selectively tough, to let comments slide off
my back when they weren't meant personally (or sometimes even
when they were), or when there was a job that simply had to be
finished. Focus on the work; process the feelings later. Now you have
two skills, two potential responses, not just one. You're becoming
"bilingual."

12. How to Pee Politely

Nobody likes Porta-toilets. They're cramped, the seats are built for giants and usually they're less than clean. Porta-toilets aren't built with women in mind. They aren't built with men in mind either, but the men put up with them because it's sissy to complain.

Your first visit to the Porta-toilet will be one of the olfactory highlights of the job. Contrary to your first impression, that small sink inside with the mothball in it, is not a sink and that is not a moth ball. The Porta-toilet does not boast a tampon dispenser on the wall either, so women have to make do, though if you're on a large site with plumbers around you might ask the foreman why the plumbers can't hook up a flush toilet. Phrase it as a challenge—"What's the matter with the plumbers on this job—can't they even rig up a toilet?" Coming from a woman, the foreman is more likely to take the request seriously. If he does, the men will appreciate it as much as you, though they'll never admit it.

Every woman deals with menstrual periods and Porta-toilets differently. I used to carry a plastic bag and take used tampons home to dispose of discreetly because my worst nightmare was of some guy staring down into the liquid tank, watching my used tampon bob around in there. They'd know whose it was.

Be creative, especially when it's raining or freezing cold and you have to take off not only your rain gear but several layers of clothes in that two-foot-six-inch space. There are now companies that make coveralls engineered for women, with a back flap.

Never be caught without toilet tissue in your pocket. On some jobs, you may have to use the bushes along with the guys. The men will be extremely self-conscious and wish as heartily as you, for a real toilet. These times make the Porta-toilets look good. On one job I was on in the middle of the city, a foreman who didn't want to pay for a Porta-toilet thought it might be a handy way to get rid of me, the first woman he'd had to hire.

"No toilets on this job!" he boasted.

"No problem," I said. "I can go around the corner with the guys."

A toilet was there within the hour. (Notice, I knew enough about the culture to take on his dare.)

Granted, Porta-toilets aren't the Ritz, but don't go for an entire day at work without using one—it's not good for your health. You're a tradesperson now; use the Porta-toilet like everyone else.

13. The Big "L": Lay-Off

It's an unfortunate aspect of building houses or bridges or boilers that eventually every job comes to an end, or needs fewer hands. Sometimes, before this happens, your boss will move you to the next job. Sometimes there is no next job.

If you're on a union job, the foreman will approach you at afternoon coffee break and give you the famous pink slip that says you're laid off, as of now. Depending on your contract, you might be paid for the next hour but you won't work it; instead, you'll pick up your toolbox and with the other(s) who were laid off with you, trudge out of the lunch shack toward the union hall to sign in for the next job. If it's a non-union job, you'll just be told to "Go home." No pink slip, no hour's pay *in lieu*.

Every tradesperson knows lay-off. It's no fun for anyone and no one ever gets used to it, even old-timers who've been through it many times. Fellow workers who were your best buddies at lunch time suddenly won't look at you, even to say goodbye, as if you have some terrible disease, as if "lay-off" is catching.

If you feel you were laid off unfairly, talk to your Business Agent. On a non-union job there's no appeal and on both union and non-union construction jobs, rarely seniority. If the boss likes you, you stay. If he (or she) doesn't, you go. Period.

Don't take it personally. Go home, have a good cry if you need one, then go directly to the union hall to sign the Dispatch List or prepare to go job hunting tomorrow morning. Enjoy your time off. In fact, if you have other interests—as I did, in creative writing—lay-off may be the perfect time to enjoy them.

14. The Paycheque

If you work for a union, the rule is that everyone gets the same hourly rate of pay: the rate negotiated in the contract between union and employer. On non-union jobs, the boss simply tells you what you're getting—usually less than the union rate.

But union or no union, hourly rates of pay in the trades are better than most women have ever dreamed. Some non-union employers like hiring women because even when they pay us less than men for doing the same job, we're grateful; it's still more money than we've been paid in our lives before. But beware: If the men on the job find out you're working for less, they won't like it. If a woman works for less, maybe the boss will offer less to the men? Don't be guilty of this. Find out (if you can) what men doing the same work as you are being paid, and demand the same. You owe it to your fellow workers. You owe it to the women who come after you. You owe it to yourself to be paid what you're worth. You're in a new ballpark now, sister; play ball!

CRANE

The construction crane grows on you. For years you take it for granted, like a mother that brings things, takes them away, does the hardest work for you if you ever stop to think about it—which you don't. Huge slings of lumber, pre-assembled two-storey gang forms, buckets of wet concrete, reinforcing steel—you just assume it will all be there with a twitch of the rigger's finger.

Then one day, when you have a moment—when the foreman isn't watching, or the crane is laying down that plywood you called for right in front of you—suddenly you notice how the rigger and the crane operator are like brothers. The crane operator runs the machine, perched in his cab, fifty feet above us all, and the rigger is the guy on the ground who directs him, ties ropes, connects the hook, tells the operator precisely where and how fast to raise and lower. He's the guy with the walkie-talkie who directs that great long-legged bird and keeps the operator from accidentally laying one of those multi-ton loads on human heads. The rigger is often the smallest guy on the job because he has to be light on his (I never saw a "her") feet, able to slip through small spaces, leap on top of loads to tie or untie, and do it all fast because people are waiting, waiting!

Perhaps they're not brothers, these two, but closer—twins. They know what comes next, read each other's minds so the rest of us can carry on blissfully below, hardly aware of tons of steel and concrete and lumber passing routinely, safely over our heads.

After a while, I decided the crane operator is the unsung hero of the construction site, unrivalled for the amount of work he (mostly "he") does and the hours he works, climbing up that ladder before the rest of us arrive, staying until the last overtime. He hasn't time to come down for lunch, wouldn't think of coffee. And when the inevitable time comes, who knows how or where he pees?

The rest of us feel secretly proud as—floor by floor—we rise past ordinary mortals in their oh-so-tidy air-conditioned offices. But the crane operator is higher than any of us, and got there first. Being closer to the heavens, and alone, he has a mystery to him. I used to wonder if he got lonely.

In fifteen years of construction work, I actually saw a crane operator only once. For some reason he was quitting with the rest of us at the end of a regular day and I watched as he climbed down the last few metal steps from his aerie, to the deck. When he turned around, our eyes locked and we both grinned, "Hi," before turning to go home.

Nothing else needed to be said. The man was Indo-Canadian, one of the few men of colour I met in fifteen years in the trade. I instantly understood his wanting to be unbothered by a crew. And he had just met the woman I was sure he'd heard lots about along the lines of, "Don't drop anything on the carpenter in the pink plaid. He's a she." We didn't need to say anything because we both knew what the other knew about being "other" in this place of white men.

Before this, the only time I'd talked to a man of colour about being in construction, was to an Indigenous guy. One day when we happened to be working near each other I asked him what he did if—when—guys gave him a hard time.

"I tell them I'll meet them out back," he said. Which wasn't an option for me.

After I met the Indo-Canadian operator, I realized there are other ways. And I always felt better knowing he was up there, a brother. Sometimes after that, when he was bringing me a load, I'd take off my bright yellow hard hat and wave. He always honked back.

How It Happened: Part I

The first time I tried on a yellow plastic hard hat in the hardware store, I burst out laughing. The silly thing perched above my forehead like a battered yellow tennis ball.

The salesgirl hurried over, calling, "It's adjustable!" And sure enough, there was a little plastic tab the two of us fiddled with, all thumbs, until we got the pieces apart, then together again and this time the hardhat fit…well, better. It still sat ridiculously high on my head so that I seemed to have a grossly exaggerated forehead. It made me nervous.

But after the first year of wearing it every day, I didn't feel dressed without it.

As a labourer on my first construction job, the foreman watched me saw through a six-inch beam with a hand saw—*very* slowly, *very* carefully—and said in a neutral tone, "My economic eyes are always on the clock." I didn't appreciate this until years later.

The first time I was working on a big crew and something didn't fit, a deep voice called out, "Get a bigger hammer and hit it harder!" Everyone laughed. But I did as he said, and from then on it became a motto, "If it doesn't fit, hit it harder!"

On one of my first days at work on a concrete high-rise, I drilled bolt holes into a concrete pad, then carried twelve-foot, four-by-six-inch wet posts to where my partner was waiting. I helped him nail them, working above my head all afternoon. Soggy from the armpits down, I could hardly carry my groceries home that night or chop the onions for supper, my arms were so tired.

Yet I loved it. I loved that I didn't have to be nice to anybody, not like secretarial where I had to smile and be nice to assholes, or housework where I'd do it and the next day, have to do it again. In construction if I'm feeling mean or mad, I just hit harder.

⚒ One day when I was told to use a hammer gun I'd never used before, the bit wouldn't stay in and I had to ask for help. The nearest carpenter was a guy called Sam who had always blasted silent but pure hatred at me. How did I know? Sam never spoke when I was around, went to great lengths to avoid acknowledging me, literally turned his back, even laughed as I passed. Around Sam, I felt exhausted, depressed, no good.

Earlier that week my partner had had trouble with the same bit and solved the problem by finding another drill with the bit already in place. But today all I could find was this one and my partner was nowhere in sight. So I asked Sam. I was an apprentice—it was his job to help me.

First he ignored me. Then he grabbed the drill, pulled the loose bit out, jammed it in and back into my hands, then turned back to his work as if furious at being disturbed. "That's not what I asked," I said, forcing myself to stay still, not to run in terror or tears of humiliation.

Sam froze. I took a deep breath and pushed on. "I want to see how it works." After a moment, he turned back and performed a twisting motion as the bit slid out and in again. He made no effort to make sure I'd seen but I had, and took it back. He'd already gone back to work. My face burned.

I wondered what he'd tell the other men when they were together tonight over a beer. "Stupid girl couldn't even get the bit into the hammer gun!" And they'd all laugh. No matter that my partner—a man—hadn't been able to figure it out earlier, either, or that someone once showed Sam how to do it, too. Girls can't do this job. I'd just proved it.

✹ "…like a library."

I wasn't sure I'd heard right. "A what?"

"A library," my new boss said again, waving his arm around at the tool room. "We keep all the tools here neat and in their place, like the books filed in a library."

And I knew exactly what he meant.

✹ The time they told me it was a board, not a log; a sticker, not a sucker; shiplap, not surfboard. How important the words were.

And even then, I tripped: once I said, referring to the rafter ends, "I'll pull mine, then I'll come pull yours." My partner took a sharp breath, almost a groan. At lunch as he examined the ginger snap I'd offered, he asked, "How hard is it?" and bit.

Should I laugh? Acknowledge or not acknowledge? Where was the line, fine plate on which we balanced? Was it true, this feeling that someone was waiting for me to fall, that we were building more than just another house together? Ah, this minuet in work boots through air that smelled like forest. We were stamping new patterns into the sawdust, dancing on both sides of the line, treading a new path to wherever we were going, men and women, together.

✹ The Carpenter's Union organized a weekend of workshops for apprentices—people just learning the trade—about health and safety issues, one of them a session on form oil. Forms are the pieces of plywood or shiplap we used to build what I thought of as jelly molds for the wet concrete. Once concrete "set"—grew hard—we'd pull the forms off, but to make it easier, we first coated them in an oil called a release agent. It turns out, the Health and Safety instructor now told us, that the form oil we were using at the time contained a known carcinogen.

"Use it as sparingly as you can," she said, "and keep it away from delicate tissue, particularly scrotal tissue."

This seemed important so on Monday when my partner, an old-timer, started to spray on the release oil, I warned him we'd just learned it was a carcinogen.

"That's ridiculous!" he said, and to prove his point, rubbed his two hands on the freshly sprayed ply, then vigorously together, as if using it for hand lotion. He dried them off by rubbing his hands on his jeans.

"She said it's particularly dangerous on delicate skin like scrotal tissue," I said.

He stopped dead, hands frozen to the side of his jeans. "What?"

Clearly, I didn't need to repeat it, and we carried on, but later that day I heard him warn another of the guys, "Watch that oil, it causes cancer!"

⚒ In 1980 we formed a Women in Trades group in Vancouver so we could lobby government and industry to train and hire more women in trades, but mostly, I think, so we could talk to each other and not have to explain how we felt at work; one roll of the eyes, one nod, and we all knew that someone else understood exactly.

We also held workshops and organized conferences where we heard great stories. One woman who lived in Yukon told us she finally got sick of barely being able to keep herself and her family alive on waitress' wages, so when she heard the local mine was hiring, she applied. She wore jeans and boots as if she was ready to start right away, but the guy in the office got a bit addled and told her they'd never had a woman apply, and had to search for a hard hat that would fit her, and he thought she should have a tour first because she might not like all the dirt. When she said that would be no problem—she'd had babies—he just looked more confused. As she told it: "We started at the top of a metal stair that had a round nose and a narrow tread. And wouldn't you know, I slipped and couldn't catch myself. My hat bounced noisily down all those twenty-seven stairs and me right after it. I got to the bottom with my bum aching and my left hip bruised but I was damned if I was going to let him know that, so I picked up the hard hat, banged it on my head and said, 'Great. What's next?' Like I went downstairs like that every day of the week, like I was just taking a short cut and what was taking him so long? After that, the tour was over pretty quick."

She got the job.

※ One day after about five years in the trade, I figured out why women don't fit—past the obvious, I mean. The reason we don't fit is that we love the work. I don't think most of us would put up with the challenges for more than a year or so if we didn't love the work. But some of the men we work with are condemned to be here because their father or their uncle did it and what else is there? So they pick up a hammer, or a welding torch. It's only the odd time they stop to think about it, like when a girl waltzes onto the job and after the first few weeks when the thrill's worn off and some jerk's needling her and *still* she loves it, then they remember—some of them—that they hate it.

And they take it out on her.

※ One of my bosses talked of "the tyranny of the tool." He meant that when a fancy new tool comes on the job (a router, a nail gun, a saw sharpener) we forget the feel, the function, the mechanical satisfaction of the older one.

※ I would have thought the men, being prone to bragging, would never acknowledge physical pain. But whenever I plucked up my courage, or forgot to feel nothing and said, "Ouch," out loud, or "It's scary to be here, thirty feet up," no one ever laughed. If I mentioned carpal tunnel or tendonitis or back pain, there was always some-one who'd nod, sympathize, acknowledge his own sore joints. They agreed easily, as if it were a relief. As if I had given them permission to discuss it and they were ready.

⅏ Once, as I was talking to the apprentice, something about writing a poem slipped out. I instantly regretted it. There were certain things I never revealed on the job, even to the guys I liked—like this apprentice. It blew my cover, made me vulnerable, showed that I was no "ordinary" construction worker after all. They already knew that of course, just by looking, but I kept trying. Was this dishonest? Trying so hard to fit in that I misled, covered up, hid parts of myself?

It never crossed my mind they might be hiding something too, might be lonely, might be hurting, squeezed thin into all the traditional macho, even violent, expectations of what is meant by "construction worker."

⅏ A carpenter once told me, "You can hide in the trades. You can talk about sports and kid the guys for years—for your whole life—and never have to say a single thing you really mean, nothing with heart in it."

⅏ Tradeswomen learn the skill of coming back with one-liners any guy could appreciate: fast, funny, and with a subtle (or not so-subtle) put-down. Heather Tomsic, a boilermaker, was our Women in Trades One-Liner Queen. My favourite:

When a guy says to you in admiration, "You've got balls!" smile and say, "Thanks. They're eggs."

⅏ Years after I'd stopped working in construction, Steve, the union dispatcher, told me that every time he sent me out on a job, he got a phone call within the hour, from the job foreman.

Foreman: "What the hell are you trying to pull on me?"

Dispatcher: "What do you mean?

Foreman: "You know bloody well. You sent me a girl!"

Dispatcher: "So?"

Foreman: "So I called for a carpenter!"

And Steve would tell him, "You wanted a carpenter? You got one. Try her for two weeks and if she doesn't work out, you can send her back."

They never sent me back. And after Steve retired, I never got dispatched by the union again. When I went in to ask the new dispatcher why there was no work—or at least, why I hadn't been called for work in months, I knew the reason within seconds—by the way he looked at me, the way he quickly turned away. By then, I was too tired of the whole affair to protest.

⅍ Sitting around the lunch table one winter day, I noticed the other carpenters' hands, pink and white and red from the cold—rarely a black or bronze-skinned hand. This is the country of white men, after all. Small hairs growing out of the backs of fingers look larger when fingers are swollen with muscle and cold. But in any weather, these hands handle the iron tools of persuasion—crowbar, hammer, screw-jack—as easily as the delicate tools of finish, chisel and plane, laying out shavings fine enough to wrap your lunch in, producing corners and fittings where you'd swear there was no seam at all. Even with arms crossed, hands at rest waiting for the work bell to ring, there's a dynamic tension to these hands, hands as springs, coiled, waiting to work. Buildings are in these hands. The nation is in these hands. My own hands look small and thin by comparison, but they too have grown thicker and more muscular since I started on the tools. Five years earlier these hands would have shocked me. Now I simply accept them as necessary to my work. They have grown with me. Working hands.

⅍ Annie Dillard, in her book, *The Writing Life,* says that in working-class France, when an apprentice got hurt, or tired, the experienced workers said, "It is the trade entering his body."

⅍ One night I thought about making love to my partner but fell asleep, exhausted, before I could do anything about it. At work the next day, at lunch, one of the guys yawned and someone teased him, "Wife keeping you up?"

"The wife can't keep me awake long enough," he said. "It's strictly sex on Sundays at our house." And I grinned into my sandwich. Partly because I wasn't used to such personal talk on the job, but mostly because I wasn't the only one who had to ration my energy.

※ Carpenters talk a lot about the weather, compare the reports on different stations, the latest changes—and it took a few years before I realized this is no light conversation when you work outside all day.

※ Next to concrete, framing was my favourite part of building. Framing is what happens after the foundation has been poured, when the structure of a wooden building, a house, begins to rise. My partner and I mark, measure, cut and place floor joists, lay the ply, and when we've finished floors and walls then it's ceiling joists, and rafters: a thinking job. We put our heads together over lumber, shoulder to shoulder over sweet-smelling wood, resin from the fresh cuts smeared on our hands like lotion as we share our knowledge of how buildings stand, of things physical.

Cutting and placing the rafters, then nailing them—commons and hips—calls for big yet precise movements, and balance. The reward is in seeing them up, wooden ribs against a blue sky, perfectly cut and fit. Usually I worked with a man, he and I separated by everything we didn't share except the one overwhelming fact of our bodies sharing the physics and sensory thrill of building. But someone forgot to give us the rules, a name for this encounter over wood. What do we call the look of delight we share, our satisfaction when the first two rafters fit perfectly—"kiss" at the ridge, the carpenters say. What do we call our unspoken, shared satisfaction in pushing through, nails driven home, a house cut and placed, one physical act at a time?

※ Looking back on my early days, I can't believe some of the conversations I tried to start. Once I asked the carpenter I was working with, "Do you ever think about time, about how much time has passed since something happened in your life? Or what if you had done something at a certain time, or met someone earlier?"

The man replied, "No. I don't think about things. I just do them."

⚓ "Don't you love that smell?"

I would only have dared say this to a carpenter who I got along with well, and this guy was one of those. When he smiled, I continued, "When I cut and the wood opens, that smell, it's like wine bursting out!" Like a crazy woman, I carried on, "Sometimes I think I'm in love with wood. It's why it took me so long to stick to one boyfriend. I'm too crazy about lumber."

My partner laughed. "Some cultures allow more than one husband," he said.

⚓ One apprentice asked a question, then another question—this apprentice asked a lot—and his partner said, "I knew you'd ask that! And I have the answer: Fuck off!" Then he gave the right answer, laughing as if it was all a great joke, as if he was passing on a tradition—which he was. Then they both went back to work.

⚓ I overheard a carpenter ask a bricklayer to cut one inch off his new sharpening stone because it wouldn't fit the old box. "In fact, can you make it seven inches?" he asked.

The bricklayer replied, "My wife asks me that all the time."

⚓ Above one half of the Dispatch Board in the union hall was a large sign that said, "Apprentices" and over the other half, another that said, "Journeymen." I was on the Apprentice Board, but when I got my Journey"man" papers—the first woman to do so in our Local—I told the guys hanging around that I thought the sign should say Carpenters.

"That says it all for everybody, doesn't it?"

There was dead silence, then one guy said, "The language doesn't matter."

"If it doesn't matter, then let's not put Journeymen. Let's put Journeywomen above the Board."

He looked at me in horror. "I'm not a journeywoman!"

"And I'm not a journeyman," I said, trying not to smirk. Amazingly, a few weeks later when I glanced up, the sign said "Carpenters."

After I left the union, they changed it back.

🎔 A carpenter once told me that when I started, some of the men were afraid. "No, not afraid exactly," he said, "just… it was 50-50 whether they wanted you here."

🎔 But they kept surprising me. Once, when I was working near the plumber, he suddenly said, "*Eine kleine nachtmusik.*"

"What?"

"That's what you were humming," he said. "*Eine kleine nachtmusik.*"

"Who wrote that?" I asked after a while.

"That's too easy," he scoffed. "Ask me a hard one. I love *Name That Tune.*"

I really had no idea who wrote it. "But who was it?"

"Too easy!" But finally he tells me, Mozart. "Now give me a hard one!"

"How do you know all this?" I asked him, reluctant to reveal my utter ignorance of classical music but curious about his apparently deep knowledge of it. All I knew were Bob Dylan and Joni Mitchell.

🎔 I was working with my friend Jacqueline on one of her jobs that called for a concrete wall to be cut. At the expected time, a small pickup pulled up in the alley and the driver got out and walked toward us.

"Looking for Jerry," the man said as Jacqueline stood up.

"Yes. Are you Stan?"

Stan looked confused. "I, ah, did you…I was talking to Jerry…," he said. "Jerry wanted some concrete cut…."

"That was me, dear," Jacqueline said, her voice smooth as glass. "You didn't quite get the name right. Or a few other things, did you?" she said, laughing now. "Follow me." And he did, as she led him to where the wall had to be cut.

I looked away so he wouldn't see me grin. As the Dylan song says, "The times they are a-changin'."

✻ It was a lesbian who told me construction men don't know women very well or they wouldn't say a very small measure is a "cunt hair."

"Every cunt hair is different," she said. And she knew.

✻ One day on a renovation job, Michael, the plumber, gave Chris, his apprentice, five dollars to buy a cinnamon bun for coffee break. Chris raised his eyebrows at the size of the bill.

"Feeling flush today," Michael explained. When the electrician overheard, it was too good to pass up. By lunch time Michael was fondly referred to by all as Flushie.

Flushie was an artist. When I passed him in the boiler room, or in what was becoming a boiler room for the heating in this new house, he was sculpting a boiler out of steel and bright orange copper pipe. His tools were neatly lined up on a tiny shelf built from the scrap I'd given him that morning. Like a sculptor under the brightness of his two trouble lamps, he was creating, "a work of art," as he told me, reading my mind. Then he added, "The perfect heat for pennies a day," frowned, and went back to work.

It suddenly struck me; here was a man who valued quality, beauty and grace as well as efficiency. He was building an object that would provide reliable heat, on demand, for many years. But more, the object itself was a thing of beauty, built with—I would almost say—love.

✻ Sometimes I think the reason I liked framing and formwork so much was because they were hidden. They're the bones of building and vital to a long-lasting house or high-rise. But once the dirt is back-filled around foundations, once plaster and paint go on, you never see them—at least from inside. The good stuff, invisible. I stuck out so much in the trades, maybe I sympathized.

ॐ It was near dusk, almost quitting time, and we were three storeys up. After a heavy rain, the air was pregnant with water, the light metallic, and the deck we were working on was backlit as if we were on a stage. Enter the chorus—hundreds of birds suddenly flying out of the west. Like black arrowheads they swept overhead in a whoosh of soprano and tenor, the sky flooded with them, right at eye height. Then just as suddenly, they were gone.

In the Beginning Was the Body

"...the animals already know by instinct we're not
comfortably at home in our translated world."
—Rainer Maria Rilke

Above all, the trades—painting, carpentry, plumbing, sheet metal work—are physical. The apprentice painter who tries to match a colour or cut a straight line like the one that looked so easy in a journeyperson's hands, is shocked to find how difficult it is. North American apprentices spend four to six weeks in school each year for four to six years, learning the theory of their trade—but it takes all that time, plus another five or six, to learn how to move our bodies and hands to apply and integrate theory with practice. The body must know.

Consider the advantages of a tradesperson. Here's someone who never has to pay for a gym. "Workout" for eight hours a day and more, is our daily routine. Thanks to all this exercise, we have more bad backs but fewer heart attacks than the general population. As a tradesperson I developed a relationship with my body that was never demanded, let alone allowed, by traditional "women's" work in office or school where I'd felt alive only from the neck up and wrists down. Instead, working as a carpenter demanded *all* of my body, demanded that I learn balance and coordination if I was going to do this well. Sometimes, if it was a good day at work, it was as if a small tape recorder in my head switched on and began to play music, rhythms I could almost dance to.

Granted, on other days it was mostly static. On my first job, or whenever I went back to work after a lay-off, the sound was mostly the whine and buzz of pain and resistance. A calf muscle calls up that it's over-stretched, my lower back screams the first time I lift a load, *Not ready! Not ready!* Feedback. I forgot to stretch before I started. So I bargain, negotiate, compromise. It's only the first day. Don't push so hard—calf relaxes. Change posture, let my legs do more of the work—back settles down with a small whimper.

This awareness of pain and physical resistance, this working through it, is a routine part of being a physical worker, but it was a revelation to me. As a girl, I was taught that if something hurt or was difficult, I should stop, or run to someone who could "fix it." Even if someone only "hurt" my feelings, I would be advised to go play with someone else, avoid pain.

But as a construction worker, where going home early means a day without pay, I learned that the need to push past resistance even if—even when—it hurts, is just another part of the job. Pain, I learned, was a physical sensation that could be pushed through. It wouldn't kill me any more than dirt would. After a while, it wasn't uncommon to come home and notice, for example, deep purple bruises on my legs and arms that I had no memory of receiving. My inner tape recorder had learned to drown out incidental knocks and strains, any pain that didn't present immediate danger—to take them as a badge of honour, even. I was a tradesworker, I could handle this.

It was a liberation; I was no longer kept busy servicing my body with bandages and rest. Ironically, I felt stronger, more confident, less vulnerable to hurt in the world at large. Often we call such behaviour "macho" and attach it to certain less-than-wise males, so it's only a little embarrassing to say I've learned to enjoy this macho. And it's not only bravado; as tradespeople, we do what has to be done, building houses, fixing things, keeping electricity, water and power moving. These are things physical, unquestionably creations of value and necessity. And so the unshakable calm, yet the modesty of tradespeople—we do this thing. It is important, useful, even vital. We get dirty doing it.

But these days we're losing touch with the physical. We drive rather than walk, use techno-tools—cell phones, text, email, Facebook, you know the list—rather than make phone calls or (heaven forbid) personal visits or letters. Would rather work in a nice clean office than get dirty using our hands at blue-collar work.

Maybe it has something to do with our North American aversion to dirt. I remember once dropping into a small café in Mexico City for a cold drink on a hot day. The owner had just taken an earlier customer's glass off the counter, and as I ordered, was casually flicking it under a stream of cold water. When I asked for orange soda, he whipped the wet glass onto the counter without so much as a pass of his dirty tea towel and, after swishing the flies from its mouth, poured soda from a half-empty litre container. Then, in a single motion and with great élan, he reached behind him to take a second glass from among the dozen that rested, open-side up, on a once-white towel. Absently, he again swung his hand through a jungle of flies, swatting them aside to fill a second glass for my friend.

I was eighteen at the time, young enough to do foolish things and delighted to defy my parents whenever possible. So, knowing my mother would be horrified, I hesitated only a second before drinking. Cavalier as I was on the surface, I was sufficiently a child of North America to monitor every ache and pain over the next twenty-four hours to determine whether I had, as I fully expected, imbibed botulism with my orange.

And an amazing thing happened: I didn't get sick. All my life, my aunties had spent routine hours scrubbing every tiny dark mark off gleaming pots and dishes. My mother, with six children, made sure her wooden floors were a miracle of wax and polish—into which I put my share of tedious labour. "Good enough to eat off!" she used to brag and certainly, those floors were cleaner than the café owner's counter. I was the obedient daughter in a good Christian house where Cleanliness with a capital C was next to Godliness. But in that tiny Mexican café I realized with shock (and delight) that furious cleanliness could now be questioned. A little dirt, I had just learned, wouldn't kill me.

Many others in the world laugh at what they see as the North American obsession with hygiene, the desire to enclose everything in Handi-Wrap. The idea of daily showers—all that water!—leaves most Europeans shaking their heads. And what's our problem with beef tartare—raw meat? *Delicieux*! Maybe because they were from the generation that didn't always have refrigeration, my aunties never let meat touch their lips until it had been fried, baked or boiled until it was grey in colour and cardboard in consistency, meat that could not harbour even the toughest germ.

North Americans are generally anxious even about touching each other. (Perhaps this has something to do with our obsession with, and fear of, sex—but that's another issue.) In many of the world's cultures, men and women routinely shake hands, embrace, even kiss upon meeting and leaving each other. Men in India and Latin America casually hold hands. Not North Americans. For us, a quick formal handshake is usually maximum contact. Too many germs. Too physical. When we touch each other accidentally in public, we apologize. As I write this, the world is in the middle of coping with the coronavirus pandemic, where not only are we asked to stay six feet away from every other human except closest family ("social distancing") but also to wear face masks, hiding facial expression and most clues as to what a person's feeling. Libraries, stores, restaurants, pubs and bars, businesses, churches, schools—all the places in which we usually connect—are closed. Too dangerous. Instead, adults and children are working "virtually," at home, relying more heavily than ever on electronic devices and computers to carry on. I wonder how much of this habit of distancing will continue, after Covid?

⅌

When I started work as a construction labourer, I began to see what I'd been missing. Our North American distaste for the physical is reflected in the fact that, when it comes to manual work, most Canadians don't even know what a trade is—except that "vocational" in high school is where the "dumb" kids go.

I left the trade years ago, but I still sometimes find myself craving that old certainty. When I first left the tools to teach construction, at the end of each day I didn't want to see any ephemeral written evaluations—I wanted to shake each student's head to see what came out. Was it a worm or a jewel? Give me some physical sign of what you might have learned today in my class!

※

There is sanity and connection in the physical. It is literally "knowing where you are on the earth," being rooted, grounded. This struck me again after I'd lived two years in a rural area without a telephone, before the days of cell phones or computers. My friends and I were in the habit of regularly dropping in on each other for visits or going out to have a coffee at the café when we felt like company, staying home when we did not. Telephone? Who needed the expense!

But eventually, for reasons of work, I had to have a phone and when I got my first phone call, I found myself white-knuckled, clutching the receiver, asking my caller over and over, "Where are you? Where are you?"

"Here," she replied, puzzled. "I'm here, at home."

Two minutes later I'd have to ask again, "But where *are* you?" Intellectually, of course, I knew where she was, but like a child who nods instead of saying "Yes," to the voice on the telephone, within two years I had physically and emotionally forgotten that technology allows us a voice without a body.

In her book, *Perfection of the Morning*, Sharon Butala writes how during a lonely time in her life, she spent years wandering alone, on foot, through the hills near her ranch in southwestern Saskatchewan in what is now known as the Old Man On His Back Prairie and Heritage Conservation Area. Increasingly as she wandered, she had inexplicable and powerful experiences in which she was moved to follow certain courses where she would stumble across unmarked First Nations' paths and spiritual sites. The land itself instructs if we will only listen with our bodies.

Butala is one of many who believe our habit of living a life increasingly detached from the physical—of riding in cars, living in cities, "paving Paradise" as Joni Mitchell put it, let alone of internet and iPhones—is cutting us off from one of the most powerful influences we have, the land. People's resulting spiritual desolation and feelings of abandonment (even when it is we who are abandoning the land and not vice versa) are reflected in a general sense of fear, loneliness, and sometimes lashing out in violence.

When I read Butala's book I'd been wrestling for a while with the contradiction that as a construction worker I was one of the people responsible for cutting trees, "paving Paradise"—and enjoying it—so I thanked her. She gave me a sense of balance, I told her, that it isn't all or nothing—we need to cut some trees to build our furniture, our shelters, but it's important we cut them, carry out our interactions with the earth and its other inhabitants, respectfully.

Butala said she now thinks this is why we, as a civilization, are increasingly fascinated by outer space. We send men and women to the moon, create movies like *Star Wars* that become objects of semi-religious reverence, see a steady increase in the popularity of science fiction as a literary genre. Our technology increasingly separates us from nature, from the physical. These days, walking along any downtown sidewalk with its "plugged in" pedestrians—earbuds inserted, reading and texting on their devices—is like walking among ghosts. The technology makes us run to catch up but running means less time to touch down, to be in touch with our own physical selves—the smells and sounds and sights of the earth we walk upon—until eventually we don't dare slow for fear of what pent-up demons might pour forth.

"We are getting further and further away from the earth," Butala told me, "to the point that our feet have almost left the ground and we are floating up, toward the stars, in danger of becoming completely out of touch." We are becoming a nation of space people.

In one generation we have gone from a culture that was impressed by an electronic typewriter ("A built-in dictionary? Amazing!") to a culture where over 75 percent of all households have a personal computer on which adults and kids spend hours, days, years surfing the net, playing games, doing homework, "communicating" without ever looking at or touching each other. People make up whole personas for themselves online, can change genders, meet and "date" without setting eyes on a living human being. The good news is that this may be one way to overcome some of the assumptions of racism, sexism and homophobia, but it comes at a price. Our e-mail addresses and Facebook and Twitter links have become vital parts of our identity instead of (ho-hum) living faces.

As author Michael Harris says in his book, *The End of Absence: Reclaiming What We've Lost in a World of Constant Connection*, "Every technology will alienate you from some part of your life. That is its job. *Your* job is to notice. First notice the difference. And then, every time, choose."

Maybe the Bible got it all wrong. Maybe in the beginning was not the Word. Maybe in the beginning was the Body, and we have been moving away from it, at our own cost, ever since.

JOB WELL DONE

In the early '80s, union work was scarce and by 1984, the union was trying to cope by dividing longer jobs that came in, into three-week segments. That was just enough to claim Unemployment Insurance and let people pay their bills—and keep a segment of self-respect. But waiting for a job to come in, then praying you wouldn't be laid off before your full three weeks were up, was terribly stressful. Even the union offered no seniority, so if the boss didn't like you, you were gone, no reason given.

Which is why, when a couple of friends asked if I would do small jobs for them—hang a door, renovate a bathroom—I decided it was time to start my own small business. I'd had a bit of experience when I was still an apprentice. In 1982, there was only one other woman in the union, Chryse Gibson, a journeywoman who'd earned her papers back East. When both of us were going through a period of unemployment, Chryse asked if I'd help her do a renovation job for a friend. It meant I could not only claim apprenticeable hours toward completing my apprenticeship, but that I could work with her and her husband, learning the business side of things.

It was a small job, putting a study in the attic and dividing a large downstairs room into two. But suddenly all the theory I'd learned in school, like how to estimate materials and the total costs of a job, was useful. I liked being in charge of my own time, my own pace, figuring out the mysteries of rooms that weren't quite square, walls that weren't quite plumb, and all the surprises, like finding a mouse nest in the walls, or historic old newspapers as insulation that you don't get when you build from scratch.

Then we kept going. There was no shortage of small jobs. We both had friends who needed things done, and it turned out that women especially, were happy to hire other women. "I feel safer giving you the key to my house," one woman said. "You answer all my questions," another said. We called our small company, Sisters Construction, because we were "sisters" in the union.

That's how I finished up the 2,000 hours I needed to complete my fourth year and get the red seal certificate that declared me a fully qualified carpenter. (Which, when it was delivered by mail from the International Brotherhood of Carpenters, was addressed to Brother Kate Braid.)

Chryse soon moved back East, but in between short union jobs, I continued to work on my own. For one job, I even hired an apprentice, another woman who'd just completed her four-month pre-apprentice training.

I'd worked with other apprentices on union jobs, most of them at third- and fourth-year levels, and now watching a first-year apprentice work—especially when I was the boss who was trying to keep things moving along—was excruciating, like watching myself in my first few months at work. I could almost see the thoughts meander slowly, one at a time through her head as she looked at each piece of lumber as if it were unique, admiring each cut.... I tried not to watch as she carefully placed, then drove, each nail, then stood back to admire it. She had no sense of the total picture, no sense of where this was all going—and why would she? She'd never been on a real job before and I'd been exactly the same. The first time I gave her a wall to frame, I made the mistake of not double-checking before we raised it. She'd laid it out from the middle, not the edge, and started her measurements "fresh" each time there was a break for a window or door, so there'd be no backing for our eight-foot-wide sheets of drywall, and the whole thing had to be redone.

That's when I remembered the first wall I'd ever laid out. Even though I'd studied it, even done it once in school—as she had—everything somehow looked different on the job, and Jac, my wise boss, had come along behind me *before* I'd nailed the studs and shown me where I'd done it wrong. When I showed my apprentice the way to do it, keeping to those critical 16-inch centres, she said, "It's just like school, I knew that!" And I remembered the same feeling—the wonder that the theory they teach you *works*, isn't just empty words, but has meaning and physical application.

While the journeyperson supervising, grinds their teeth.

I told her not to worry. I'd made similar mistakes and she'd make lots more. Mistakes meant she was learning. And again, I remembered Jac's almost desperate (though still polite) plea to, "*Please try and go faster!*" It had had no meaning at the time but now I got it. I'm sure that's one of the reasons employers hesitate to hire first-year apprentices and I know it's why, on later jobs, my first hire was always another skilled carpenter, most often Jacqueline Frewin, who in turn hired me when she needed another hand.

Renovations was an entirely different world. Instead of reporting for work and doing what I was told, now there was only me. I did the estimates then made the bid, presented it to customers and when it was accepted, had to find, interview, organize and schedule sub-trades (plumber, electrician, sheet metal worker, drywaller…), pick up materials, prepare the site, and coordinate timing and materials for sub-trades. It was a heavily administrative job as well as a hands-on one, doing the carpentry work myself—and all through it, keeping in close touch with clients who'd drop small bombs like, "Oh, didn't I tell you I changed my mind about those cupboards? I think the new ones are a little bigger…."

Nothing seemed straightforward. When you've contracted for a while, you develop a whole crew of sub-trades who know you and are ready to work for you. But up until now all my contracts had been very small and increasingly I needed a more committed and larger group. I was starting from scratch. When I was looking for an electrician, for example, the first man I called, whose name I'd found in the Yellow Pages, stopped just short of sneering when he met me. He barely looked at the plans, the existing fuse box (once he found it), then quoted what seemed to me an enormous amount of money for a small job.

In the absence of experience, I relied heavily on some very traditional tools—my feminine skills of intuition and body language—and nothing about this guy felt right. So I got crafty; I told him I'd let him know, then checked the Yellow Pages again. This time I looked for a small ad, suggesting a company that would offer more personal service without a big overhead, and (forgive me this bias), I looked for a European name. European tradespeople in those days trained for seven, not the standard North American four years. And when Ivan Andreassen (a Danish immigrant) turned up, he was utterly respectful, asked all the right questions and gave me a quote for the job that seemed reasonable. He got this job, and he and his son, Per, would do all my electrical work for as long as I was a contractor.

Often in those early days I was crazy with anxiety—what had I forgotten?—so that I came home at night exhausted before grabbing a sandwich and working on the next estimate, phoning the tile setter to tell her we were ready for her, etc. To help me organize, I bought one of those new-fangled things, an answering machine, so I wouldn't miss calls. I was barely making a living, paying everyone who worked for me a higher hourly rate than I was making, but slowly, as I got into the rhythms of it, beneath the worry and responsibility and hard work, I began to enjoy it. I was renovating a bathroom, a basement—organizing plumbers, electricians, cabinetmaker, a lino layer—to create more beautiful spaces for people. By the winter of 1984 I could write in my journal, "I am a woman contractor/carpenter, working steadily. Do you not find this amazing?" I began to think of the women in my professional life. I had a woman doctor, a woman dentist, a woman accountant and a woman lawyer. This was indeed the Old Girls' Network and I wouldn't be working without it. This is how men had thrived for years. Boldly, I added, "I will thrive too."

In the spring of 1985, I started my biggest job yet—a large addition to a house in Burnaby that would require excavation, concrete foundation, framing, roofing and interior finish—the whole works. For this, I'd definitely need a skilled carpenter and I started asking some of the men I'd worked with in the union. The first five I asked, none of whom were working at the time, all said no. So though I knew she hadn't done concrete work before, I called up Jacqueline who immediately said yes. At least I had a willing carpenter.

When I later asked one of the five men why the men had said no, he said the problem was that I'd told them I wanted someone to work "*with* me," when I should have said, "work *for* me." He said he was afraid that if he accepted, he would have had to keep bailing me out, or that I'd want long emotional discussions and he just wanted to be able to, "do the work and get on with it."

And here I'd been just trying to be honest about having a working relationship where we could talk about the work as it went along. It was that female "trying to create community" habit, getting me into trouble again when the men just wanted a boss to give orders.

There were problems. On day one, when the backhoe operator was taking longer than planned to do the excavation for the new addition, I went out to pick up supplies, leaving him the pump I'd rented in case of any water. I also clearly marked the location of the main water line. When I returned, the customer's back-yard was a swimming pool. The pump was broken. The mechanic I then called to fix it told me that this wasn't just leakage—the backhoe operator had broken into the main water line. When I confronted him, the operator simply turned away, ignoring me. Was this my mistake? Then I caught the mechanic rolling his eyes. Next time, I scolded myself, I would assert myself. Deep breath, and on we went.

Neither Jacqueline nor I had ever done a job of this size before, but she was a careful, hard worker and increasingly I relied on her.

The actual concrete pour was intense. Jacqueline's job was to hold the eight-inch hose that fed the heavy, wet mix into the forms. She did it just fine though in a very non-traditional way, standing on top of the forms and holding the pipe, with its thick, gushing liquid, between her legs. "Better for my back," she said, when I laughed.

It was incredibly phallic, and I noticed that the men on site—concrete truck driver, pumper truck driver and concrete finisher—all sturdily avoided looking in her direction.

It was clear that none of the tradesmen I'd hired had ever worked with a woman carpenter, let alone a woman contractor and *two* women carpenters. My original order to the local lumber yard was done over the phone, but once the job started and I began turning up in person, clerks at the order desk froze when I walked in. It took a few weeks for them to start offering the contractor's discount without my asking. I guess they figured anyone who comes in at 7 a.m. for her second 50-pound box of spikes that week, might be more than a householder, even if he is a "she."

Then there were the inspectors. When Jacqueline and I finished the foundation, I needed a plumbing inspector to confirm that our concrete had been sufficiently waterproofed before we could back-fill the dirt over the drain tiles and start framing. On Jac's jobs, inspection had always consisted of a quick glance at the walls—black tar coating the outside, gravel covering drainage pipes to the right depth—and the permit was quickly signed.

On my job, the inspector might have been inspecting a nuclear facility. He hummed and hah'd and retraced his steps, walking around the foundation several times. I was holding my breath when he finally said, "It's bubbling."

What?

He'd noticed that the thick, black tar coating we'd painted over the foundation to waterproof the concrete, had bubbled in a few places.

"A possible entry point for water," he said, looking fiercely disapproving. Hadn't seen bubbles like that in all his twenty years in the trade, he said.

I'd seen exactly the same bubbles on Jac's jobs, so I jumped in the ditch and popped several bubbles to show him that underneath, it was still tarred, still waterproof.

Not good enough.

He made Jacqueline and me completely re-tar the foundation and I gritted my teeth while he did a second, almost equally thorough inspection. This time, he couldn't find a single thing to criticize.

His thoroughness was later almost matched by that of our final building inspector, who—when the house had been framed and was ready for lock-up—did a breathtakingly thorough inspection that started with creeping through our crawl space with his flashlight, inspecting the spikes in every single one of the joist-hangers. But that was later.

It was shortly after this, that I made some comment about construction being, "men's territory" and Jacqueline replied firmly, "Kate, this is your territory now." I wrote it in my journal, a precious reminder.

And now came our excavator to do backfill. I was leery of this guy—after all, we'd had that small problem of the unplanned swimming pool. So I'd wanted someone to be around, but Jacqueline had left for the day and I had to run to the hardware store. I left him with a clear reminder that the Building Code specified that the top of backfill had to be eight inches below the top of the concrete foundation.

"Yeah, yeah," he said, dismissing me. And I tore off to the hardware store.

When I came back, he'd backfilled to within three inches from the top of the foundation. When I insisted he remove the extra, he agreed—then handed me a bill for his extra hourly work.

When he came the next day to pick up the second cheque, I told him I wouldn't pay him for removing the extra dirt.

He was a tall man, and heavy. When I said I wouldn't pay him, that it was his responsibility, he came close, then closer, eventually roaring in my face, "You owe me money!"

But I'd remembered a women's assertiveness technique called The Broken Record and I tried not to shake with fear as I used it now.

"I'll pay you for the backfill, but I won't pay you for removing the extra. It's your responsibility."

He continually cut me off, his face getting redder and redder, shouting. "You owe me money!"

"I'll pay you for the backfill but I won't pay you for removing the extra. I'll pay you...."

I was shaking, and sweating, but determined. I wasn't going to tell him that I'd made a few mistakes of my own and was already overbudget on this job. I couldn't afford to pay him extra for his mistake, too. "I'll pay you for the backfill but...."

Finally he gave up, and stormed off. Jacqueline came out of the house and gave me a hug. "You were brilliant!" she said. But I'd been terrified.

Luckily, I'd just been to a lecture by the fierce American feminist, Andrea Dworkin, who'd said something along the lines of, "If you take power from someone, you have to be prepared to watch them suffer. You will hurt them, and must be prepared to handle that." After the lecture I'd asked her, What do you do about your femininity, your identity of yourself in traditional terms, when you're doing non-traditional work? And she'd answered, "There has to be more ruthlessness, less asking and smiling politely."

The next day at work, Jacqueline—a proud lesbian who, unbeknownst to me, had been at the same lecture—said, "I knew that was you asking that question, Kate. You're such a Fem!" She said it in that half-teasing, half-affectionate way that lesbians use when they call each other "Dykes." I took it as a compliment and we both laughed.

Jacqueline had become my stalwart ally, my backbone on this job. When we started, she'd seen me freeze up with uncertainty a few times when confronted by the homeowner, an engineer who watched everything we did like a hawk, and came home from work early every night so he could ask endless questions. Every time he questioned something, I'd been in the right but not confident enough to insist on what I knew. After the second or third of these incidents, Jacqueline made a casual comment about, "Maybe if he's looking for a bitch, he should find one."

And I got it. The next time he questioned what I'd done, I practised more of that same assertiveness and he backed off, even apologized saying he hoped I wasn't offended that he asked questions, he was just very interested.

One month later, the backhoe operator took me to Small Claims Court. Our client had been fascinated by this entire episode. He'd been at the house and witnessed (from the shelter of his kitchen) the yelling part. Now he took time off work to come with me to court. He'd read the Building Code, seen the high levels of backfill, and was as certain as I was that we'd see justice done.

But though I showed the judge the picture I'd taken of the over-filled foundation, and the Building Code that specified eight inches of clearance, the judge didn't bother looking at the Code, just leaned down and said in a patronizing tone, "It looks to me like you owe this man some money."

My client was as incensed as I was and insisted on paying the extra cost himself.

It hit me in the middle of screaming out loud in my truck as I drove home, that I wasn't going to quit. This wasn't easy, and yes, I'd made mistakes (that measurement on the height of the foundation walls…) but neither Jacqueline nor I had ever done anything this big before and we were doing it now. Doing it right. Mistakes were inevitable. Isn't that what Jac had told me, what I'd told my first apprentice? What's important, Jac had said, is how you fix them. And I started to grin. Was I crazy? I *liked* this? Yes. I was learning an enormous amount. The worst that could happen was that these owners would fire me and never recommend my work to anyone else, but someday I'd find another addition, and do it better. Me and Jacqueline.

The following week when we were lifting the main wall, a long, heavy one, I asked the plumber if he could give us a hand. At one point I caught him looking at me carefully, almost appreciatively, and I saw myself: red undershirt—my favourite one that *just* showed the curve of my breasts but no details—beige jeans, grey socks with a red stripe holding close my pant legs, heavy work boots with holes in both toes, my hands on my hips as I talked to the owner, excited about having all my walls go up so quickly. I felt strong, competent and in charge. But during the lift, there was a moment of confusion and I could feel the plumber start to take over, give orders. And I simply spoke louder, gave *my* orders, and took back control. It felt good, felt right. I think I might not have been able to seize that initiative two years before, but I was doing it now.

When we finished that job, on time and (almost) on budget, the same building inspector who'd gone into the crawl space to check every detail of our nailing, signed the permit then shook my hand. "A pleasure working with you," he said. "Job well done." Indeed.

MAKING MUSIC

In the beginning is quiet; the fading song of birds finding shelter elsewhere, steady bass of a carpenter's heartbeat as her shovel bites earth. She is checking for the bones: drainage, foundation, gas lines, water. She bends, bows to what is to come.

A wild heartbeat greets the roar of the digger—a warmed-up violin-gone-violent sound of steel on rock scraping over the going-going-gone! of old concrete, cracked patios and ancient stairs. The air horn belches and farts, tooting over earth until finally five o'clock brings relief and the deep silence of stopping. Then, echo of a hammer, lonely, from somewhere down the block. Do neighbours know that tonight they should listen hard before the resonance of this space is changed forever?

On the morning of the first day, re-enter the carpenters, conductors of construction about to make a modern music. The home-owner brews an extra pot of coffee, bakes cookies, to the children's delight, as a lunchtime offering. And now—can you feel it?—the high-fidelity clatter of a tool belt. "My apron" the carpenter says, lifting it to her hips, settling. Click of the silver buckle and a touch to the hammer—just checking. Hands full of nails, an iron rain into her apron. A pause as paper plans whisper, hum as the carpenter decides what, where, how. Deep breath before the plunge.

Now, stereo of boots on earth as steel-toes approach stacked wood, sudden zest of the perfume of lumber, then the *thwuck, thwuck* sucking sound of two-by-fours rising wet off the pile as the carpenter moves her wood around, getting the feel of her material, saying *Hello! Welcome!* The first machine sounds are a blast, the fast buzz of a clean cut. And it is begun.

Now her hammer sings with the pounding of spikes in a tim-pani-drumbeat assertion of order, her steely command over the chaos of lumber and dirt. Listen! The timbre of a twenty-two-ounce hammer sings from ear to groin to toes, lifts, shifts, focuses on that spot where the next spike will meet the wood it has been waiting for. It is a masculine sound of success, achievement, victory. It is a feminine sound of reunion, completion, wholeness.

Penetration sounds start deep in the grain as a change in reson-ance. The carpenter listens for it, knows the sudden thickening tone of satisfaction—wood to wood. There will be rhythm, as two-by-fours and two-by-tens dance the dances they dreamed when they were still tree. Hammer and nail and lumber glory in their union. Wood rises, erect and shameless. Nails sing their way into cedar and fir, hemlock and spruce, joining with a different tone, different col-our to each, *thwack* of a juicy smack into wet wood, a much politer sound into dry. Here are the sounds of size, of delicate two-inch nails as opposed to their big tough cousins the spikes, of cranky galvan-ized and finicky Chihuahua-hyper finish nails.

Harmony of laughter, the rising pitch of voices getting ready for concrete.

Concrete has a symphony of sounds to accompany it as befits such a heavy customer. Deep breath of anticipation as the truck snorts its way along the alley, revving up to hoots and roars as the driver manoeuvres its bulk, lets down the chute and the first thick shovels of stony concrete roll down, a gravelly roar on steel. Then intensity, sharp cries and the giant's dinner as everyone rushes to serve the needs of this beautiful monster before it turns everything to stone. The carpenter shouts, *Shovel! Shovel!* Grunts as labourers, carpenters, everyone sweats and runs. Scrape of gravel and sonor-ous sucking sounds as concrete floods out of wheelbarrows and into the forms—she hopes. Dull clunk as wheelbarrows hit and miss. Curses. The concrete truck driver watches it all, silent. He's conspicuous—the only one on this site who stands still.

Only after concrete lies tranquil in its forms and it's all up to the patient scrape, scrape, scraping of the concrete finisher does a carpenter welcome the wet of the washing of her tools, tuck steel pins into the hardening mix to hold the house down, send the apprentice for Slurpees, extras for the children watching. Sucking sounds of satisfaction: Piña Colada and Orange.

Now a pause for the intermission, rest, a weekend away, then under the sounds of wood come the sounds of sub-trades: percussion of sheet metal and pipe and the swish of glue. When she hears the grunt and scream of the chain saw, the carpenter runs; this plumber cuts before asking.

The carpenter is contractor, is conductor, so other trades perform to the wave of her hammer, which is why she calls them sub-trades. (This is a totally unobjective point of view.)

Electricians consider themselves the intellects, nerds on the site. Nothing heavy, please! The whining of drills is a necessity and embarrassment forced on the apprentice, but after, there is only the quiet of wires unravelling, connections being made, mathematics and the liquid surd of power and light.

Almost over, and now comes a slow stream of neighbours-getting-curious sounds, *thump-thump* of the carpenter's hammer inside skeleton walls, bass beat of keeping this show on the road. With the finishing trades come high white sounds as the drywall finisher administers the final touches, sibilance of screw guns as cabinets are hung, tiles pressed into place by a woman in red coveralls. Then comes the slap of paint, first flush of the toilet and finally carpets are laid. Take your shoes off! It's almost over.

Goodbyes are terribly sweet as carpenters slip into the deep sigh sounds of packing, tool belts easing onto dirt, tap and rattle of odd bits of lumber, sawdust, rusty nails tossed in the dumpster, patches of paint that were once desperately important. All that's left is the scratch of a pen on the final paycheque, cold click of profit and loss, the acoustics of *Goodbye! Goodbye!*

Parents have mixed emotions. This carpenter has made their lives more ugly and more beautiful at once. When she is gone, only the children will be sorry. It will be so silent without her.

A New Dance

When I enter the hall, intensity hits me like a physical thing, like walking absent-mindedly onto carnival grounds and being suddenly shocked by bright colour and motion, the smell of excitement and danger, something slightly forbidden—smell and sight and sound. The hall is noisy with loud dance music, low light and movement. It's filled entirely by women.

And I'm afraid. What might happen in a place full of only women? As if somehow I am safer, as if the air is diluted, muted, in the presence of men.

"I'm buying." Jacqueline says. "What would you like?" and for one crazy moment I feel like I'm being offered anything my heart desires. "What would you like to drink?" Jacqueline repeats and the bubble bursts.

"Cider," I say.

Jacqueline rolls her eyes. "Oh, think of something more dramatic!"

And suddenly I'm drowning again, breathless, like a new swimmer putting all my faith in the coach's hands.

"Scotch," I say. Is this me? "On the rocks."

"Much better!" And my building partner disappears in the direction of the bar. I try not to feel anxious, not be too wide-eyed at the forms of women, only women, around me. I feel suddenly very, very conservative. What legends and lies have I heard, listened to, believed even, that I should feel nervous in a room of my own kind? Not a conference room—I'd been at lots of women's conferences—but a dance, in low light and a freeing of day's ties.

The woman directly in front of me has a ring in her nose and wears a red, almost see-through patterned dress. Beneath it are pink tights. I try not to stare at her nipples, colour coordinated with the outfit. The woman is busy talking intensely to a small Asian woman with huge gold hoop earrings who wears a black body stocking and tight black pants. I feel like a foreigner. I feel like I did the first time I went to England, knowing we all speak the same language here (don't we?) but hardly understanding a word. My clothes, that seemed just right when I left home, now strike me as absurdly reserved.

I'm saved by Jacqueline who returns with the drinks and suggests we dance. I've danced with a woman once in my life before—slow danced like this—at a women's bar in Winnipeg at the Women in Trades conference. But Jacqueline's body is different—bigger, stronger. She laughs when I automatically take the woman's position, my right hand in her left, my left hand on her shoulder.

"Of course!" she says, taking the man's position and almost literally sweeping me away. She laughs again and spins me around. I want to sit down. I want to watch a whole lot more before I take part in any of this. But then I spot someone I know, another tradeswoman, and it's like a lifeline. And the music creeps into me. This body that at first felt like the tin man in Wizard of Oz, clanking and stiff, slowly lets the sweet oil of music seep in and I relax—a little—and let music take over, my body, my muscles, finding themselves, coming loose, dancing.

Jacqueline seems to know everyone, greets everyone, kisses several of the women as we dance past. It's as if, by coming here, we've crossed a threshold. By day, we build houses together. By night—this night—we've entered Jacqueline's other world, the world of women who love women, and it's suddenly clear that I'm here under her charge, her care. I want to catch her eye, want her to talk to me, bestow on me some token of acknowledgement, but she ignores me, dancing with her eyes closed, humming to herself.

When we take a break, I meet a woman I know, and then another. Jacqueline has disappeared and so I dance with whoever is here—more easily now.

The music is a mixture of Motown, blues and reggae. If I listen to the words many of the songs have a strong political focus, but increasingly, I let the music wash over me like a tide, letting my arms and legs and body move with their own motion. It's several hours later before I go to find Jacqueline, dancing in a circle of three other women. Her eyes are closed and she acts as if she is quite alone, her face glistening with sweat, her dark silk blouse clinging.

I have to touch her shoulder before her eyes open and slowly focus.

"I'm leaving."

The fine hairs on her upper lip, her cheeks, glisten wet.

"I'm going," I repeat, louder. Jacqueline's eyes focus now but she doesn't stop dancing, hips and shoulders moving with the music as she speaks.

"See you tomorrow," she says, slow and lazy, as if she's been smoking opium all night, immersed in a private dream. She closes her eyes again.

When I leave, I step carefully over women spread like warm butter across the front porch.

How It Happened: Part II

One night after twelve or so years in the trade, I dreamed I was leaning against a funeral bier. It was like a fairy tale. On the bier lay a child, semi-comatose, waiting for something. I was reading the kid a bedtime story, only forgetting words, skipping pages, and it didn't seem to bother me that I was doing such a rotten job. Beside me was a woman, the child's mother, entirely wrapped in veils. Every time I finished a story, she took off another veil until—when I came to the last story, a poem I remembered from my childhood—she took off the last veil and there was nothing there. I could see right through her.

We were on a hilltop and just behind us was a tree, blasted and gnarled and twisted by some invisible wind. The tree had no bark, no leaves, no flowers. All the beautiful, living parts—the places for birds to play and wind to sing—had shrivelled up, been stripped away. What was left was the absolute core, the heartwood. But even that was wasting away, growing weak, barely hanging on.

The next morning, I knew the tree was me and I was seeing the price I'd paid over the years, how the leaves and bark, mother and child—my feminine parts—had twisted, shrivelled or at least gone to sleep and only my pith, my core, my heartwood was still standing as I struggled to fit, to prove myself to the men, to myself, to show everyone a woman could do this. And I *had* done it, *was* doing it.

But a tree needs a forest.

I began to think of leaving this trade I loved. Even a little female was wildly extravagant in a forest of men.

ℳ Was it around this time that a guy on the job told me that in the mythology of the Jains (a sect in India), people's needs were supplied by 'wish-fulfilling' trees?

ℳ When I was working in northern BC with Indigenous men from the Tahltan Nation, it took me a while to understand I was with people of a distinctly different culture. I really liked my first partner, Scott, but at the end of each day, he disappeared without a word of goodbye. One minute he was there, then he was not. One day, annoyed, I asked him why he never said goodbye. He looked me in the eyes and patiently replied, "If I got nothing more to say, why say it?"

"Right," I said. And he left.

ℳ At the end of my first day working with George, my second Tahltan partner, he hung around and watched while I cleaned off my hand saw, ran wax paper over the saw and tape measure blades, and packed everything carefully into my wooden tote box.

"Where'd you get that box?"

"I made it." I was concentrating on getting my toolbelt to stay inside. "It was the first project in pre-apprentice class," I said, only half paying attention. Then I looked at him. George was staring at my toolbox with an emotion—was it longing?—I'd never seen in him before. It was the first time I'd seen myself through his eyes, the enormous privilege of my life, taking for granted the right to train for my apprenticeship, a white woman—a woman, but still—white woman among other white people, in a building built (I was sure of it) by white men, administered by white men for the sons—and very occasional daughter—of other white men. Not an Indigenous person in sight.

I looked again at my toolbox—a simple oblong with a round handle and small divisions for saw and level and pencils—this simple box that looked so amateur to me now, years later. But George was staring at as if it were a wonder. To George, I realized, it was a symbol of what he later told me he so wanted and couldn't have—training for his chosen trade, among his own people, in his own place. What was so wrong about that? Until that moment I'd always taken my ethnicity, my skin colour for granted, though my right to be a carpenter was a little rockier. Maybe that's why I could read him now. "I want that too," he was saying with his whole body. "I want to be a trained carpenter, too."

✷ Someone, perhaps it was at a party, told me to my face that I couldn't be a carpenter, that I was only doing the job because I "just wanted to be a man."

He was wrong. I didn't want to be a man, though I loved some of the things men love. I loved building things, being outside in every weather. I loved to feel my body, strong. And I loved to feel I could look after myself. Are only men allowed these things? In a world where every quality has been designated either male or female, why must I pick and choose? Why can't I be both—both strong and tender, intelligent and emotional?

"But what about the difference?" people say, nostalgically, as if our differences will save us. Why are we so obsessed? For fear of some revelation? What if the differences finally topple and beneath them, we find we aren't so different after all? What if the so-called differences are just a way to make sure one group of characteristics—gender, race, sexual preference—can dominate the other? What makes one "better"?

✷ One day when a bunch of us at Women in Trades were discussing pin-ups on the lunch shack walls, one of the lesbians joked, "I have a better chance of sleeping with that pin-up than any of them." Another added dryly, "I don't think it's about sleeping. It's not about love."

"What's it about then?" someone asked.

"It's about laying her out on the wall to look at. It's about her not being able to reach out and touch them or ask anything of them. It's about her being under their control."

✻ At another meeting of Women in Trades, there was a long discussion about whether it's old men who give tradeswomen the most trouble on the job, or young ones. There was a pause, and someone said, "Both wrong. It's the short ones."

✻ One day heading home after work after a particularly long, hot, hard day, I was grimy, sweaty, red-faced and stinky, wearing an old black T-shirt with a ripped sleeve, scuffed steel-toed boots and a yellow hard hat. An ironworker passing as he left work said, "We want a sex kitten on our crew too."

When I hissed at him, he thought I was joking.

✻ I have to admit that in some ways, working with men was an escape from women. I'd felt with most women that I had to be a bit careful, hold back, not try too hard. It was contradictory because I also loved to be with women. But somehow with women I felt a bit guilty when I did well.

With the men, I could forget this careful self-control, this non-competitive competition. I could try as hard as I possibly could, do my utmost best, and feel joy in the doing because the men were usually doing the same. And there were always a few who knew more than I did, usually the older ones who'd been doing it longer and who didn't resent my learning. Those were the ones who taught me.

If I did the work, then, unlike dressing up and looking pretty and balancing on high heels in a bar, the reward in construction was in seeing my own handiwork out there in front of me, for as long as I lived. Building a house was far more fun than cleaning one.

Trying to explain this to Jacqueline, why I was now going back to work for the union with an all-male crew, I guess I like the differences, I told her. I *need* the sameness of women, but I'm intrigued by men, their rough honesty. I can't understand them. Or else they're easier to understand. Even to me, it didn't exactly make sense. I just knew I missed their roughness, their camaraderie, the joy of building *big* things.

❦ Sometimes I surprised myself, when I was feeling good on the job, able to crack jokes. On one job, the foreman (who everybody heartily disliked) said to me, "I thought I'd see you in a mini-skirt rain outfit, with a big slit up the middle." And I growled back, "I'll wear my mini when you wear your kilt." And everyone laughed—amazing!

❦ Another day the same foreman had told us the wrong way to build something. When the superintendent questioned it, the foreman blamed us carpenters, saying, "There are bad journeymen on this job!" I replied, "But excellent journeywomen!" To which the superintendent replied, smiling, "And bad journeywomen too!" But by then it had become a joke, so every time we spotted the slightest error or imperfection, someone would say, "Bad journeyman!" Until one of the guys grinned at me and said, "No, bad journey-*person*!" and after that the joke was, "Bad journeyperson!" And we'd all laugh.

❦ On that job, we all got nicknames: I was Koff Drop Kate because I always coughed (from what I later found out was an allergy to wood dust) so I carried cough drops I liberally passed out to anyone in my vicinity. The foreman was Louis the Lip, and Roger, a labourer who was extremely slow, was Rigor Mortis.

❦ Carpenters have a wonderful quiet confidence. "No, we've never done that before," they'll say, "but we'll figure it out, we'll build it." And they do. *We* do. (They also call this "bullshit," but most of the time there's something solid behind it, and if there isn't, the foreman figures it out pretty fast!)

❦ One time a guy I was working close to, bragged, "When I do the floors at home, I do 'em the way I want to do 'em. I'm the King of our house."

Someone else picked it up. "Right. The wife tells you what to do and you tell the kids."

All of us within earshot, smiled. And the hammers didn't miss a beat.

✁ I asked one of the labourers, "How are you today?" and he said, "Life is a bitch and then you marry one."

✁ Over the years I very slowly—on some jobs more than others—became one of them. Or at least, I could see what was going on. For example, one day in the shack before work, the new guy asked when payday was.

"Didn't they tell you?" someone said. "On this job you work the first month for free. On trial." And before the new guy could respond, someone else said, "Yup. And in that month, you have to give up smoking, drinking and sex. Otherwise…."

Then we all laughed, and the new guy laughed too, nervously. We all knew that for a moment, he'd bought it. A one-up on him. Welcome to the crew.

✁ Once, I told one of the on-the-job jokes to a woman who asked me, "How can you live with that misogyny?" And I told her about the good times, the crew times when I disappear as "woman" and "Other," when we're all high together on sunshine and productivity and building. In those times, I told her, I've seen their vulnerability, their tenderness. And I understand them as men far better than I ever did from merely knowing a male friend or lover. This joy of doing physical work together is one of men's best-kept secrets.

✁ The more I see men at ease in their inner sanctum, at work, and the more I am accepted and at ease with them, the more I suspect that a lot of the standard misogyny is pure fear of us women as foreign, un-understood. Most of these guys have never spent much time in women's company, never been able to talk to us in a language they're relaxed and comfortable in, just as we women are seldom comfortable talking to them. We don't know each other, so we mistrust each other. Then all other things being unequal, we also come to fear each other. How can we bridge this gap?

✳ One day I look at my crew and realize they will never approve of me, never. No matter how good a carpenter I am, no matter how good I get at their jokes, their talk, their way of working, I will never be one of them. And I don't care. All those years of trying, and suddenly I don't give a shit. I'll do it my own way and be lonely, but to hell with trying to please them. I won't do it anymore.

Now if only I could have held on to that feeling on every job....

✳ On one high-rise job, I began to wonder if the safety officer was gay. This was in the 1980s when coming out as a gay person could be downright dangerous, and in construction, unheard of. And yet...? This man was always careful to say, "Ladies and Gentlemen," when making an announcement or starting a safety meeting. He was the only construction worker I'd ever seen who actually touched other carpenters. I was suddenly aware that no one here ever touched another, except when they had to, to boost them up a wall, or get their attention. And this guy seemed to genuinely love his work. For example, lately he was very concerned about getting a safety belt that would fit me—and incidentally, the smaller men.

Later I wondered if I'd been here too long. As if any guy who loved this work, who was thoughtful and touched anybody else, had to be gay. I worried I was getting cynical.

✳ And speaking of differences, the only time I ever had a black foreman, I was a little uncertain at first of how it was going to go. On my first day on his job, he was very chatty, wondering out loud why a woman would want to be a carpenter, and then, "This is hard for the men, you know!"

That was a new one.

"They," (he said "they" not "we,") "can't talk shop anymore or put up their pin-ups."

I'm not sure what gave me the courage with a foreman, but when he said that, I lost it.

"Pin-ups are sexist," I said. "They're just another face of racism," daring to name the obvious. This man, of all men, should know better. "And do you really need pin-ups in your shack?" But he didn't walk away, and our conversation went on until he said something about, "Women keep joining organizations."

Then I got it. "Is your wife a feminist?" I asked.

"Becoming one," he said. It worried him a lot.

Then my partner joined in. "Those feminists shouldn't be allowed," he said, "breaking up marriages and everything." Which actually gave me another perspective on why a woman on the tools, like me, might make some men very nervous.

In fact, over the next while I came to like Ovid, the new foreman, a lot; I liked his humour, his fast way of getting a job done, his obvious skill, the way he lightened things up on the job. With Ovid around, there was even the odd conversation in the shack about family things that made me remember men don't usually do this at work, like when I asked him about his kids and he turned, after, and asked one of the other carpenters—in the funniest, very uncertain voice—if *he* had any kids. And these two had worked together for years!

✻ I appreciated Ovid even more after he left the job to build his own house; it was as if he had in some way protected me, and now the gloves were off. Suddenly Keith, my partner, and Joe, our labourer, wouldn't talk to me. They talked *only* to each other, which was very weird considering a labourer is supposed to do whatever the carpenters tell him—no questions asked. At one point, Keith said we should get a handrail on the man-hoist shaft we were working close to, for safety, but then he started talking to Joe, not me, about how to build the wall near it. Neither of them so much as glanced at me.

I said to Keith's back, "So what about the handrail?"

He said, "What handrail?" and looking only at Joe, rolled his eyes.

"You're not thinking again, Katie. It's a wall we're building here. There's no handrail!"

After a few days along those lines, I went home one night and wrote carefully in my journal, one round word after another, without thinking: "Now I understand why men invented the Medusa, a female monster with a beautiful face and hair of coiling snakes, who turned men into stone if they dared to look at her. Now I understand how their terror of us women can go so deep, they need this kind of horror to explain it."

Why are we so unknown, so hated, so feared, so needed?

But when I looked it up, I found that Medusa's name in ancient Greek means "guardian" and "protectress." Guardian of women, perhaps? I started to think maybe Medusa *liked* turning men into stone. Perhaps she notched her hammer every time another one froze, made a point of changing one per day into statuary—just for the exercise. Maybe her front yard was full of stony men petrified into blessed silence. Perhaps she was thinking, like my grandma used to say, "If you can't say something nice, then don't say anything at all." I was beginning to see the Medusa's point of view.

⁜ Things weren't going well, either at work or in my relationship. One night John and I had another fight and that night, sitting up alone, I drank too much red wine. Somewhere toward the bottom of the bottle I stared at it, thinking, "I could pour the rest of this down my throat and it would splash, like pouring wine from one hard glass bottle into another." I felt like a hollow log. No—a log holds moss and shelters beetles, fertilizes the forest floor. I was only a hard, crisp ceramic exterior with a glazed smile. Sunlight would glint off my hard surfaces. I felt like an empty vessel waiting for filling. Or breaking.

⁜ On it went at work, with Keith and Joe ignoring me or making pointed comments for days, weeks, until I felt like a mad woman, not to mention a stupid one, and almost yearned for a lay-off. What had I done wrong? What was I being punished for? One morning as I came up to our workstation, they actually whispered to each other, "Here she comes!" Like boys.

On that job, the intense relief of Friday nights was matched only by the intense preparation that went into getting myself ready to work again on Monday morning. Sunday night I'd think "work," and feel my mental heels dig in: *No! I don't want to!* Feel myself almost physically being hauled toward that site. *Don't want to! Don't make me!*

I began to understand those men who don't like this work but do it anyway; it can numb you. Sometimes you have to numb yourself or you'd be too scared, too angry. The question is, What choices do we all have? With a few university degrees behind me, I could quit, go write a book, or become a teacher or a bureaucrat. Most of these men didn't have that background, had never done anything different, couldn't imagine it. I began to understand the deep-down resentment I'd only sensed before, that sometimes there's no pay that's enough pay.

✻ Fooling around at home with Lao Tsu's famous *Tao Te Ching,* I opened the book at #28. It starts, "Know the strength of man, But keep a woman's care." And later, "Know the white, But keep the black." It reminded me of the issue of balance in this workplace that—until now—hadn't known any.

✻ Sometimes I tried to imagine what it would be like to have another woman on the job, to glance over at another scaffold and see a woman there. Then I'd wonder, "What does she think of it all? Is it awful for her on some days too? What does she do when she has her period? We're the same in this." I wonder if she'd be just like another guy to me. Would I like her? She, me? Would we have special lunches together, find a place where we could meet and talk—really talk—about the guys, the work, how hard this is, what our partner said this morning? Would I feel relief that another woman shared my distaste for the pin-ups? But what if she didn't? Would I feel nervous that she might react in what I thought was the "wrong" way, making it harder for both of us? As we each struggled to fit in, would the presence of two of us make that impossible? Or more possible? What new metal might be forged in this smelter?

※ The real problem with being unhappy at work, dealing with difficult men, was that I came home and dumped it on my part-ner-now-husband.

"Quit!" he'd say, over and over. "If you don't like it, quit!"

"But I love it!" I'd say through tears. "I love the work!"

It was all so confusing.

※ "Courage is the first essential." — *Katherine Anne Porter*

※ Unpleasant as it was, the combination of Keith and Joe at work didn't deeply shake me until one day when I was working alone, finishing up some bracing beside the elevator well. I was enjoy-ing the peace and quiet, not paying much attention to the noise of someone working above me—Joe, as it turned out—when I turned away for a second to reach for another piece of lumber, and a heavy, pointed pry bar came hurtling down onto the deck and landed exactly where my back had been, seconds before. I looked up at the three-inch gap in the plywood deck above me and saw Joe, looking down. He didn't say a word.

"Joe, you could have killed me with that thing!" I yelled. I was furious but still, Joe said nothing. When I saw him later, he muttered something about "clean up." That was all. But later, as I was back to working with Keith, I bent over, an instant before I heard the sound of a hammer hitting metal right above my head. When I straight-ened, Keith was staring at me with a very strange look.

"Good thing you bent down," he said, and looked over at Joe. I realized then, the sound had been Joe's hammer. He'd been swinging at a piece of metal scaffolding but missed, let go of the hammer and it had arced across the spot where my face had been two seconds before, hitting the jack beside me. Coincidence?

That's when I reached my limit, and all of us knew it. For the rest of that afternoon we did things *my* way, no questions asked. Keith was a lamb, and Joe stayed away entirely.

The next day, I was laid off.

℀ I wasn't sorry. In fact, by this time I wasn't even sure I liked heavy construction, or not as much as I'd once thought. After this long in the trade, and with the last few years often spent on smaller renovation jobs working with women (and men who had no problem working for and with women), I was thinking maybe I preferred the smaller scale.

That job with Keith and Joe was the worst I ever worked on, but the next was one of the best. It was another union job, heavy construction again—a major renovation to a Burnaby mall—but what was different was the crew, including the foreman, and my partner, Eddie. I'd worked with Eddie a few years earlier when he was two years behind me in his apprenticeship—which helped now with my authority, since Ed generally liked to tell everybody the way to do everything. But he was always willing to discuss it, to listen, to bend. Then there was Larry, a soft-spoken guy who, when I mentioned I'd once taken a finishing course with the job foreman, said, "He only has Grade Six, you know." As if it mattered. As if maybe Larry did too. And for the first time I wondered how much my obvious education—my vocabulary, my way of speaking—irritated, intimidated, threatened them.

On that job there was also Chan, who I knew from our mutual activism in the union and who burst out laughing when he saw me, delighted to see a union sister. His delight might also have had something to do with the fact that he was a man of colour—another outsider. And there was John, who told me his wife had seen one of my poems printed in the Carpenter's Union magazine, and Fred, who practically insisted I use his saw when we ran short. A whole crew of decent guys and a good foreman. What a difference!

I soon realized another difference. I hadn't started in construction until I was thirty-one, but now, after thirteen years in the trade I was at the stage most of the men around me had been in for ages because they'd started sooner. What I realized was that I *knew* this work now, knew not just how to do each job, but how to approach it. I may not have done this particular job or used this particular bolt, but I knew that if you showed me, I'd know. And if you didn't (or wouldn't) show me, I'd figure it out.

It was confidence. It was cockiness. It was even arrogance. I didn't have to rush around and prove myself anymore because I knew I could do it. Bluffing? No problem! It was almost fun to have this blasé-ho-hum-what's-next sort of approach. I was a carpenter.

✼ This was the job where I'd never had such a clear sense of the smoothness of a well-run site. I was working a lot at heights so all day I could see plumbers and labourers, electricians, rodmen, foremen walking around below, moving steadily, doing what had to be done. There was a lot of metal work on this job—over there, the forklift hoisted red steel beams to an ironworker in striped overalls and blue hardhat who walked out onto the beam he'd just attached, pulling out his spud wrench and screwing a huge bolt in to weld it. The scene below and around was occasionally lit by the eerie flicker of welders' torches. I loved that quick nod of the head where a welder flips forward his (her?) mask as she bends over a thin line of what looks like fire as it flashes in front of her. Those flashes of light were everywhere on this job—as if we were replaying moments from a movie, *Flashdance* live, almost romantic.

Don't tell anyone I said that.

✼ But you can't afford to get romantic on a job, not for a second. A few days later our foreman was climbing the same scaffolding Ed and I had climbed a thousand times. But he was in too much of a hurry, slipped and fell back onto uncovered rebar. He hit his head, his elbow, and had a two-inch puncture wound in his butt that would need five stitches. They lifted him out by crane in the garbage box, accompanied by the First Aid attendant.

✠ When young women asked what it was like, I'd say building was like sewing, or knitting, or any of those crafts usually done by women. You take separate pieces, separate colours, shapes, sizes, and put them together until something grand and different comes out of it.

Once, a young woman I'd said that to replied, "I don't sew." And another tradeswoman jumped in. "Do you know Bingo? Construction is like a huge bingo game," she said. "There are verticals and horizontals and diagonals of wood and sometimes steel, and you add or change them all day into different combinations and shapes and sizes."

The young woman giggled. "Where are the numbers?" she asked.

"The numbers are us, the carpenters. And the electricians and plumbers, the tradespeople. We move in and out of the spaces. When enough of us get together in the right combinations in the right space, the game—the building—is finished and we start another one."

The younger woman laughed. "You make it sound easy."

"It is. Sort of," the older woman said. "Once you know what you're doing. The hard part is doing it, figuring out how to build a certain shape or how to persuade a large piece to go in a small space."

Or how to persuade your work partner to let you do the work, I thought.

✠ Working with all men or sometimes all lesbians, I often felt in the middle, and on the bad days, on the edge. When yet another man asked, "What are you doing here?" with his eyes, I could feel my heels skitter toward the edge. With the women, a voice in my head kept chanting out of nowhere, "But I *like* men! I *like* men!" No place, I thought, has to be someplace too.

✳ I love to feel strong. One day, working on an extension to the Vancouver General Hospital, we had to extend the scaffold which meant lifting up two more sections, and my first impulse was to hold back. "I can't!" And maybe a year ago I wouldn't have, would have waited for a labourer to come along. But today I was feeling good, work going well, so I went up top to raise them myself, by rope. And it felt great. As I balanced on two planks, thirty feet up in clear air, I watched my muscles swell and ripple beneath my skin as I moved. It was even better to glance over and see two labourers—in between emptying concrete buckets—watching. I knew they were impressed. I am beautiful and strong!

✳ One day on the bus heading home, I noticed the man sitting across from me looking at my feet, so I looked as well; two very large, very faded brown leather boots with the steel showing through the scuffed toe of the right one. They were laced high with bright red laces tied double around the ankle. Thick work socks with a (matching) red stripe around the top were pulled up over my jeans to keep them from catching on rebar or anything else that might pull me down or trip me.

I looked up at the man, who caught my eye and looked away. I grinned. A working woman's shoes.

WHICH WAY FROM HERE?

Four years after I thought I'd left construction for good, I had a new passion—writing—that arose directly from the notes I'd been keeping every night after work for years. I'd taught construction at the BC Institute of Technology for two years, and for two more, worked in administration, giving trade unionists access to university programs. But it was killing me: stuck indoors all day, glued to a desk and a schedule, worrying about detail, detail, detail—I knew I couldn't keep doing this. Already I'd published two books of poetry and now I wanted to spend time—*all* my time—writing. I started by going back to university for a master's degree in Creative Writing, but I needed cash to finish my second, final year. Knowing no better way to make money fast, I nailed down a summer job working for a contractor on a major home renovation.

In the first week, I tripped, banged into things, my foot went through a rotten floorboard, and I finished the week in glorious fashion by cutting through the main water feed to the house. I slunk home just as the plumber arrived to fix my mess. After four years away, I was moving too fast. I'd forgotten the rhythms and pace of this work.

How you move on a construction site says a lot about your skills: how you walk, carry materials, set up your work area, how you handle tools. The care and attention you show, what I can only call "grace," are your real credentials, the reason no one ever says, "Show me your trade school certificate." They know it just by watching how you move. And moving at a careful (but quick) pace on a construction site isn't just so you can look good out there. How you move is critical to your safety and the safety of the people around you.

But my body quickly remembered, and in the second week of work, Roy, the boss, put me to work with his long-time carpenter, Terry, and with Peter, the apprentice.

From the beginning, Terry, the carpenter, treated me with a sort of concentrated distance, avoiding any interaction with me. By now my radar was pretty good and I figured Terry wasn't thrilled I was there, but he was smart; he knew this was only for the summer so he wasn't going to upset the boss or in any way threaten his own job by complaining about "the girl," no matter how he felt. Which was fine by me. I knew this would be my last job in construction and I also knew—once I remembered the moves—that I was good at it. I had nothing to prove and for the first time, didn't care what these guys thought of me. I'd just do my work, collect my pay, and go back to school in the fall. Besides, I'd never asked men to actually welcome me, just to work with me, and Terry seemed willing to do that. So I'd thought my sense of unease around him had been my lack of confidence because I was so clumsy.

Or maybe it was my swearing. Years before, I'd worked in a treatment centre for what were then called "emotionally disturbed children," and the kids taught me how to swear. It had served me well in construction. On most jobs I'd been on, but not all, the carpenters routinely swore. But some men were sensitive about it, especially if it was the woman swearing. So on this job, the first time I let slip a casual, "Oh God!" Terry said, "Name dropping again, eh?" The implications of this unusual response passed right over my head until another time when I happened to swear, "Jesus!" as Terry walked by, and he said, "No, just Terry." Then I got it; he was a religious man who wasn't into taking the Lord's name in vain. So I tried to curb my tongue. When I asked him outright if my swearing offended him, he said, "Not me. But it bothers Peter here," pointing at the apprentice.

I almost laughed out loud, it was such a classic construction guy response: "What? Me care? I don't feel a thing!" The apprentice looked totally surprised and it was clear who was bothered.

That night, I thought again about how differently I felt on this job from any I'd had before. I knew it was my last time on the tools, and I was only here for the summer. I was also confident that I could handle anything I was asked to do and if not, I knew I could figure it out. I didn't need to impress these guys or prove myself.

Still, I tried not to swear.

But there was something else bothering me—the slow smell of trouble from Terry. I wondered if it was his own insecurity, the fact that he wasn't physically very large. He was about my size, in fact, and about my age. Maybe he felt threatened by my strength? I put my finger on it after a trickle of comments about women that turned into a steady stream. One day someone was tearing down a nearby house and as we sat at coffee there was an odd sound like a huge popcorn popper going off. For the past hour I'd been nailing hurricane ties into the tight spaces between joists, using little taps of the hammer because there was no room to get a good swing, and when we heard the popcorn popper sound Terry said, "It's twenty-four women with tiny hammers."

It was actually funny, but it was the fourth or fifth crack about women that day and it was still only 10 a.m. I was getting tired of this. Then I caught him telling the apprentice a dirty joke; I got there just in time for the punch line, something about a cat falling in the water, "and that's why things get wet when the six inches come out."

The apprentice just looked embarrassed. It was as if Terry, the older man, experienced carpenter, was trying to male-bond but young Peter wasn't that kind of male. Or not yet. So why was Terry doing this? I'd seen it enough in the trades that I wasn't really asking; I knew. I was making him nervous—a woman doing his job? In the past I might have worked hard at understanding him, soothing him, just getting along. But not this time. This time I shared the attitude of all those guys I'd worked with to whom this was just another job, no big deal, so let's get on with it, overlook our differences and get the job done.

But Terry wouldn't stop. The last straw was when he and I got into a silly strength competition firing a load of garbage into a bin off the back deck, where he pushed me, macho-like, to work harder, faster, faster.... Until it wasn't fun anymore, or safe, and impulsively I snapped, "Fuck off, Terry!" Then, both a bit shocked, we slowed down and finished the job in silence.

The next morning, to my amazement, he brought his four-teen-year-old daughter to work, "To show her around, introduce her." And after that, he treated me better. Why? I could only guess he was one of those guys who doesn't know what to do with himself when a woman arrives on the job. I'd met lots like that before. But this man was clearly a proud dad who knew how to act with his daughter around.

Shortly after, the boss asked me to show Peter, the apprentice, how to build a complicated set of rafters for a fancy ceiling struc-ture inside one of the rooms. Terry started working nearby, listening closely. When my first set didn't fit—I'd forgotten about a change we'd made after the initial measurements—Terry stepped in to help by holding the rafters for me to nail. And somehow things were just fine between us after that. Maybe because he saw I really was a carpenter—rafters are one of the most complex things we do. Or maybe he saw that I could accept help, so from then on it actually felt good (some days) to work with him.

This is what I had done for fifteen years; over and over I'd tried to outguess the men, to figure out what they were thinking so I could get around their fears, so they could just relax and work with me. I'd always assumed—I was sure—it must be all about gender. It rarely, if ever, crossed my mind they might just dislike me, that we weren't getting along as people. I couldn't seem to separate me/per-son from me/woman, couldn't escape the comment of a guy who, when I'd asked him years ago why he'd been giving me a hard time, said, "It's nothing personal, just that you're a woman."

One day when I was working late, the boss stopped and asked how it was going with the guys. I knew he was asking them the same about me. Luckily, I could say by then that I liked working with them. I was honest, said I'd noticed Terry, the carpenter, was a bit uncomfortable at first, which I figured was because I was a woman.

The boss said, "It's more likely your credentials."

What?

Like many carpenters, Terry had learned his trade on the job. But I'd turned up with four years of apprenticeship training, Red Seal papers, fifteen years on the tools and experience teaching construction—the official stuff. Now I understood one of Terry's early irksome comments about, "So, you're a *paper* carpenter!" The boss told me that whenever he brought on a new carpenter, someone with papers, Terry's confidence would plummet, and his work would get worse for a while.

I'd had the same confidence-dropping experience with foremen or anyone else on a job who clearly didn't like me. And that answered my question; it *isn't* always gender. Lack of confidence happens with guys, too. Why was I surprised?

After a few weeks, I got partnered with Peter, the young apprentice, and we had a great time working together. When the boss announced a while later that he was changing us around again, this time putting Peter to work with Terry, both Peter and I were careful not to react. The boss watched us carefully, then said, "No, I meant Peter, stay with Kate." He watched again. What did he see? Both of us had been careful to simply nod assent. No feelings. I'd always wondered if there was any psychology behind foremen pairing up certain carpenters to get the most work from each of them and now I was sure of it. The boss had read the body language—if Peter and I enjoyed working together, then he was bound to get more work out of us, with less hassle to him. I felt like a researcher on my own job. I could put pieces together now that I'd been too emotionally involved with to put together before.

I was delighted to keep working with Peter. And embarrassed, because I knew by now that I was a mole, a spy inside the world of men, sabotaging this young man's mind by working in an outrageously non-construction-worker-like manner, because we talked.

All day. Worse, we didn't bother with the usual topics of cars and sports but talked about increasingly personal things.

I'd never done this in my construction life before. Never dared, afraid to step out of line, to not fit as a "real" carpenter. But this time I didn't need to convince anyone else. I was confident of my skills and interested in just enjoying working with this young man who hadn't yet been inoculated into the usual male construction worker ways of acting, the traditional construction culture. So Peter and I could hardly wait for the day to begin before we started talking. At first I wondered whether it was just me, then I watched his face, how open it was, how much conversation he initiated with me compared to how much more careful he was with the others, the men. One day, he even asked me about my writing, something I had never, ever, mentioned out loud on any job. How did he know? I was suddenly very quiet and he—clever young man—likewise fell silent, giving me time while I suddenly had to go find something, anything, else-where, before I dared answer. When I came back, I told him about the glazier's comment the week before, when he'd said his hearing was so bad from never using ear protection that going to concerts was like watching musicians behind glass, almost silent. And how I'd made that story into a poem.

Peter simply nodded. "Nice," he said.

We were breaking all the rules. It made me want to cry. It was as if, for fifteen years I'd walled off a core part of myself and now found this young man quietly taking down the barriers to join me on the other side. We could be simply "people" together, regardless of gender. He reminded me of my son, of the young men I'd taught construction at the British Columbia Institute of Technology and how important it was to catch them before they learned the rough rules of what it is to be a "real man" on the construction site—or anywhere else. How they can learn to accept a woman as an equal, a teacher, even a leader. Sitting with Terry, the carpenter, and Peter, the apprentice, at coffee that day, I felt as if I were looking at carpenters past and future—or what I hoped might be past and future—a future in which the way people get along on a job is simply to accept each other as human beings.

A few days later at coffee when Peter and I were alone in the house, he told me his father had died when he was thirteen, so he was pretty much raised by a single mum. This explained his openness, I thought, his willingness to respect the leadership of a woman, the fact that he wasn't afraid of me. I'd only ever met this before in men raised by women, and in Indigenous men who came from a matriarchal culture. They seemed more accepting of women, more sensitive—or maybe just more willing to let others see their sensitivity.

Working with Peter, I also started to allow myself to work out loud. I'd never done this with a male partner before, and mostly it was for my sake—I think most clearly when I can do it out loud. But I also knew it was a great learning experience for an apprentice. I'd learned so much on my first renovation job, listening to Chryse, the journeywoman I was with, think out loud beside me. Talking out loud, Peter and I were working this job out together. I used him as a third leg, for balance, so he felt an important part of the process. It also made me feel even more confident about my work.

Then one day I turned up for work feeling like a phony. Who did I think I was to think I could do this? But Peter came in to work revved. I ignored him for an hour or so, just focused on getting the work done. And Peter took over, initiating all the next moves. I knew he wasn't saying, "I'm better than you." He was just thrilled that for an hour he could lead, and was relieved that when a problem came up, a building decision had to be made, he had someone there—me—to take responsibility.

After an hour or so I was over my snit and again took the lead, but it had been fun watching him. How sensitive and yet unspoken is the intimacy of working closely with a partner. What a lovely thing is apprenticeship, this process of learning by watching, by doing, what a satisfying, successful way to learn—and teach!

That Friday, tired of the endless heat, I found us something to do on the main floor where it was ten degrees cooler. We were both balanced on ladders, bending to measure, fit and nail reinforcing between ceiling joists so the drywallers would have lots of backing. I was acutely aware of my body. In four years away from this work, I'd forgotten the pure joy of being physical—the rhythms of bending, cutting, lifting—the work getting done, everything going well, my body a smooth, efficient machine. Most of the time that physical pleasure is expressed by any carpenter as exuberance: a joke, giving another guy a hard time, bending in to work even harder, faster, a whoop. We all know it means, "This is fun! I'm feeling good!" but no carpenter would say it out loud.

Nor is there any physical contact, short of a slap on the shoulder—though very occasionally, when there's just one more nail to put in or a single brace to add to a top plate, carpenters will support each other against a wall with their hand, one supporting the other's bum, creating a sort of seat while the other nails. It only takes a minute and saves having to go for a ladder. The first time that became the obvious next step for me and my (male) partner, we both froze. I turned to look at him, clearly thinking the same: Were we going to do that "bum" thing?

"I'll get a ladder!" I offered a little too quickly—and didn't wait for his answer. I knew he'd be relieved.

Now, as I worked with Peter, there crept in that old sense of the joy of the physical. I was having fun. As I passed the nail gun, I dared to let my hand touch his and felt a sudden, unexpected, unmistakable jolt of the erotic.

I froze.

Here I was—the trusted senior, knowledgeable teacher—and I could see the enormous potential for sexual harassment. How tempting is a young, vigorous body, the innocence of someone learning your trade, dependent on you, admiring of your skill and know-how. It was something I'd only ever understood before from the woman's side but suddenly I was understanding it from the position of the one in power.

I pulled back, and from then on was careful to avoid physical contact. The impulse didn't need to be followed up on. Still, it shook me. I had just seen the line that so many men had crossed with me, with other women, over the years. The line they still cross.

I'd certainly known that some things cross that line without being physical at all, like the language. It's something women in trades talk about, how part of the tension of this work is in how every word has to be watched. Perhaps because there were never (before) any women around, men in construction in North America use an often-sexual vocabulary: there are "studs" to "erect" and everything that sticks out is a "nipple." We measure "the depth of penetration" of nails, and plumbers use "ball-cocks." There are "male," "female" and even "lesbian" electrical connections. The tool you use to be sure fresh concrete is well settled in the forms is called a "vibrator" and yes, it looks exactly like a huge dildo. (Luckily for me, on my very first job on the island, my kind boss put me in charge of this job and called it "puddling.")

After a while I'd got used to this language, even bold enough to use it occasionally, usually without thinking. One day as Peter and I were strapping a ceiling and the question was whether we should break the two-by-four on a joist or carry it through, I asked, "Should we go all the way with this one?" And inwardly froze. But I didn't follow it up with a hasty rewording as I would have four years earlier. I just waited.

Peter didn't blink. "Yes," he said. We weren't talking anything sexual with each other, but it was another breathtaking leap of faith that we could play with such language, confident the other would take it the right way.

This was a new way of seeing myself, not just as carpenter, but as carpenter *and* woman. Where was this new line, new balance? How do we speak of the grace and harmony and pain of two people sharing hard physical labour without shortcutting to sex? Peter knew I liked him, and vice versa. We also both knew, without saying it, that this was strictly a working relationship, intimate without being sexual.

I'd felt this intimacy occasionally with other men, men I'd really enjoyed—no, loved—working with, and who seemed to enjoy working with me, though always before, they'd been the senior carpenter. Was it just coincidence that they were also always very good at their trade, that what we shared—this "love"—was of the pure joy in building something fast and well together in an intense, physically dangerous context where we were also looking out for each other as partners?

Still, reversing roles and gender was breaking new ground. How do we define physical pleasure between sexual beings, when it isn't sexual?

The construction earth trembled.

FOREVER AFTER

What I Learned From the Men

※ I learned brotherhood. Not just because I became a credentialed member of the United Brotherhood of Carpenters and Joiners of America, but because I learned how to walk, talk and think (sort of) like them; that is, I learned *what* they think, but I was never entirely clear on *why* they thought it. I learned to accept they just did.

※ I learned my trade. I couldn't have earned the Red Seal Certificate that marked me a fully qualified carpenter, couldn't have run my own renovation business without men who were willing to work with me and teach me—particularly Ted Bowerman, Jac Carpay, Heron Douglas, Colin Boyd and Cal (whose last name I never learned). Also Bill Zander and many of the men in the Carpenters' Union. They loved the work as much as I did, respected the trade above all else.

※ And the trade itself? I learned the mysteries of why a building stands, the power of triangles, the beauty of rafters and stairs, the sorcery of a framing square. It was magic, what we did. I will always be grateful.

※ It took two or three years to learn the culture, including that sarcastic humour with which men defend themselves and quietly duel. The point of it for most men is hierarchy: Who's the quickest? smartest? strongest? *Wow! What a man!* For me, who was mercifully *not* required to compete, I eventually figured out how to make those one-line, slightly cynical, slightly mocking cracks that meant I was one of them, even if I was a bit odd-looking, but still, on most crews,

I became one of the team. I talked the talk.

Although after I left construction, I had to learn how to severely monitor when and where I applied this skill. Years later, in one of my first classes teaching creative writing, one young man made a wisecrack in class and instinctively I came back with some of my best "carpenterese," putting him subtly down, making other students laugh at him. I could tell by the shocked look on his face, this was *not* what he'd expected. So I learned to reign myself in. (P.S. He was an angel and a staunch ally for the rest of the term. So the technique worked there, too.)

≋ At first I put the men's bluntness down to a lack of emotion. Later I realized it wasn't that they didn't feel, just that they didn't *show* their emotions the way women do.

Behind a construction worker's bravado is fear, though they'll try mightily not to show it: not fear of heights, sharp tools, being laid off or you-name-it. For most men, their fear seems to be of making themselves vulnerable in front of other men. In the end, I think that becomes a weakness; it means they can't ask for help, don't dare to. *What are you anyway? Some kind of wuss?*

On the other hand, the men taught me you don't always *need* to show emotion. We're here to get this building or bridge up and there's something clean about just getting the damn job done; head down, ass in the air. The important thing in the trades is that at the end of the day, you can see what you've done, and exactly how well you've done it. There's no hiding on a construction site. If it was a good day, you can be deeply proud. Though of course, you'd never say it.

≋ Construction taught me to stand on my own two feet. Literally. As a woman I'd learned to be aware of my body mostly as a thing to be looked at by others—mostly men. As a secretary, I was aware of my body from the wrists down; as a reader and scholar, from the neck up. But in construction you have to be aware of *all* your body—starting with where your feet are.

After a few months' work as a labourer, I went into the city for a women's conference, where one of my lesbian friends asked if I'd become a lesbian. "You carry yourself differently," she said. Mostly this made me wonder about the differences, why straight women aren't entirely comfortable in our bodies, while lesbians are.

People tell me today I seem "grounded." Yes. I learned it in construction.

⁄⁄ Construction workers don't talk much, or at least, nowhere near as much as any group of women I've known, so I had to learn to shut up. It took a while to figure out that using fewer words makes sense when you're constantly moving and using loud equipment, in a hurry to get the job done. So there's a bluntness, a get-to-the-pointness of much of the conversation. As one foreman said to me, "If you prefer talking to working, you can go home and do it." This is hourly work—he didn't have to add that if I went home, I wouldn't get paid that day.

⁄⁄ I learned patience. One entire day, as an apprentice, learning to hang a single door? And even then, the latch wasn't right and had to be redone. But oh, how beautifully that door swung when I was finally finished!

⁄⁄ I learned that men and women—by whatever our own definitions—at times need our own separate gathering places without the other gender(s) present. Though we can learn to get along, to respect each other's differences, there are still real differences. I know from my pleasure at—and need for—all-women meetings like Women in Trades, and the consciousness-raising groups of the '70s and '80s, there are things I can say and do that only women seem to instantly "get" in a precious, "You too?" moment. These are the times when I can let my hair down in a way that's difficult to define, that I cannot do so openly with men in the room.

✳ For years men have had construction as (yet) another male-only club—and I came to appreciate the shock for some of them of a woman being able to do "their" work. I know from talking to men training to be nurses that it can also happen in the reverse, that a formerly all-women's workplace can struggle to accept the first man. But as women move into the workforce—out of need, out of desire, out of a current desperate shortage of tradespeople—I learned that the workplace is no longer appropriate as a men's-only club.

And I learned—years after leaving construction, while reading Sam McKegney's interviews of Indigenous people, *Masculindians: Conversations About Indigenous Manhood*, that Indigenous societies acknowledge male companionship in some interesting ways. In the traditional Iroquois nation there were all-male warrior societies, yes, but being a warrior wasn't about violence or creating fear. The word "warrior" translates as "carrying the burden of peace." So according to Daniel David Moses of the Delaware First Nation, being a warrior meant "maintaining the good rather than participating in war." And "macho"? In a workshop on how to end violence against women, Marlin Mosseau, a senior Lakota man, said, "When the Southern Cavalry invaded our communities, our people were just appalled by what they saw, which was drinking, rape, swearing, rough behavior."

✳ I learned from the men in construction that not all male teasing is sexual harassment. And I learned how to tell the difference. The clearest way I've heard it explained was by Warren Cariou, a Michif (Métis) man who teaches at the University of Manitoba. "There is a certain othering element to teasing, but I think it's actually a performance of, not welcoming exactly, but sort of bringing a person in…. I know when I'm in an Aboriginal community," he said, "if I'm not being teased, I think here's a problem. Once you're being teased, you've been welcomed in a certain way." This kind of community-building is also used by men in construction. It took a few years, but eventually I came to understand it, that when the men teased me, I was "in."

✻ It was John, my partner, who pointed out how every time some-one said or did something on the job that hurt me emotionally, I got upset. There was lots of crying in the first few years. Mine. "Don't take it personally!" John said a thousand times. And a thousand times I echoed, "How can I not take it personally? They said (or did) it to *me*!" And cry some more.

Until I got it. One day, working on a downtown Vancouver high-rise, I was a journeywoman with my own apprentice—an ap-prentice, I later learned, who was such a poor worker, no one else would work with him.

An apprentice's job is to do what their journeyperson tells them. Period. But this guy had his own ideas. Finally, when I'd asked him twice to help me carry a heavy sheet of form ply and he'd answered that first he had something else to do, I blew. Oddly, I wasn't really angry. I was just impatient, so I *acted* angry, cursing and swearing and threatening to tell the foreman he was a lazy bum. The journeyman working close to us happened to be a gentle soul who looked over, shocked—he'd never heard me talk like that. But inside, I was perfectly calm—this wasn't personal, I just wanted to get the damned job done.

And an amazing thing happened; my apprentice snapped to attention, grabbed the other end of the plywood and practically carried it on his own to where I pointed. For the next few days he couldn't jump quick enough when I asked him anything. And I understood; this was why foremen could yell at guys for not doing something right, then all go off arm in arm for a beer after work. They didn't take it personally!

It was an incredibly useful tool not just on construction sites, but in the rest of my life. Someone giving you a hard time? Ignore it. Don't let it get to you. Just get on with what has to be done and don't take it personally. It saves an awful lot of stress and worry.

✻ The men taught me to use what's at hand to just get the job done. If you've run out of two-by-fours on the deck where you're framing, you let the foreman know, then go straight to work on another part of the job until supplies arrive. Just don't stop working!

And by the way, don't complain. You can whine all you like to your fellow carpenters, but never if the foreman's nearby. Even if a problem isn't your fault, just get the job done and move on. No one likes a complainer.

✳ Once the men on a crew accepted me, once I felt less visible, I learned there's a softness, a rough tenderness, a love even, among people who trust each other physically, with their lives. This too, is part of the brotherhood. You know these men will look out for you, do whatever they have to, to keep you—and them—safe. After a while, it has nothing to do with you being a woman who "needs looking after," because you don't. This is about teamwork, about camaraderie. About "brotherhood" in its universal sense. In this way, construction was healing to me as a woman; I learned that men too, even in this rough trade, feel deep emotion, only it's buried a little deeper.

✳ But—apart from when I did my own contracting or worked for Chryse or Jacqueline—I was always the only woman on any job. And it was lonely. I knew I was being constantly watched, that somehow I represented all Womankind and if I couldn't do this, or do it "right," it proved no woman could. As long as there's just one woman (Indigenous person, person of colour, one LGBTQ or you-name-it-not-straight-white-male person) on a job, we remain outsiders, the Other. Researchers know this. In *Men and Women of the Corporation,* Rosabeth Moss Kanter reports that at a level of less than 15 percent participation, women (and all Others) are tokens, to be ignored. Only when we reach around 15 percent do we become "a minority"—a significant, if small, percentage of the workforce that must be paid attention to.

In 2020, women are still less than 5 percent of the Canadian and American blue-collar skilled trades. We have work to do.

Constructing Language

People who know me as a writer who's published several books of poetry and non-fiction, and taught creative writing for several years, are surprised when they find out I was also a construction carpenter for fifteen years. To me, the connection is obvious—vital, even—and the transition, organic, though until now, unspoken. So how exactly *did* construction lead to becoming a professional writer?

I've always loved language. Through high school and university, I studied English literature and especially loved poetry—the physical roll of it on my tongue. (That should have been a clue—the physicalness of it was also what I first loved about construction.) One day in a university Chaucer class, the prof, who tended to overindulgence, turned up drunk. Instead of a formal lesson, he spent the next two hours reciting *Canterbury Tales* in the original Olde English. I was mesmerized. Years later, the language of men in construction was almost as unique: one-liners, always one-upping the next guy, with extra points to the man (or eventually, woman) who could make it funny. It was as much a form as any sonnet.

But when I applied for that first job in construction and the men encouraged me to "Lie," about my lack of experience, it was what I as a writer would later call Fiction. On a construction site it's considered its own work of art, though I didn't know that yet.

The fiction of my building credentials worked. But even then I could see the parallels—writing, meant building individual words into whole sentences, lines, poems, the same way a carpenter puts together pieces of two-by-four or plywood, and with nails and skill and effort creates a house. It's all structure; only the materials are different.

But being a construction worker was more than just the work; there were the guys to figure out, and having no other women to talk to about this strange new culture, I'd turned to journaling. As a kid I'd kept a small pink diary but now, every night I came home and wrote three and four single-spaced pages about what had happened that day, trying to make sense of it. Writing gave me not only a concrete product but a way to figure out—and let go of—what was on my mind. Writing still does.

There were other similarities: in construction, tools are vital and you pay the most you can afford for those that will serve you long and well—much the way a writer carefully picks the next computer, even the colour of her stickies and notepads. One of the things I'd loved about construction was its intensity; one wrong step and you could hurt yourself badly. But poetry was intense too, took all my focus. And if I did it right, at the end of the day my work was beautiful. I could say, "I built that." Oops, I mean, "I wrote that." But mostly, I liked it that construction—and poetry—slowed me down, made me pay attention.

There were differences, of course: construction paid better—much better—and was far more physical and more sociable, regardless of what I sometimes thought of the company. But the work was physically hard and the hours long, especially after I started my own renovation business, so my journaling grew steadily more condensed until one day it struck me that my entries (mere "notes" by now) looked almost like—could it be?—poems.

Tom Wayman, my first writing teacher, became a mentor: it was Tom who invited me into his writing group, the Vancouver Industrial Writers' Union; Tom, who told me I had enough poems for a book—unimaginable as that was at the time; Tom, who helped me put together *Covering Rough Ground*, which won the Pat Lowther Award in 1992 for best book of poetry by a Canadian woman. Later, it amazed me that other women asked me to come read and speak about my experience as a carpenter. As I wrote, I'd been thinking only of other tradeswomen, but it turns out women in construction aren't the only ones who get lonely and are isolated at work; here were women accountants, architects, students, lawyers....

I never planned to be a carpenter or a writer. For that matter, I never planned to get married either, but I did that too. I often doubted myself—still do. But with that first book, I was launched, and it was construction that got me here and that continues to feed me. You never know how one passion will carry you to the next.

POSTSCRIPT: WOMEN WHERE?

During World War II both my aunts were Rosies; Kathleen, an inspector in aircraft construction, Kelly working in the cafeteria at the same plant. For most women, this was the first time they'd worked outside the home and many have spoken with pride about how they loved the work, loved the income and the independence. When the war was nearing its end, women took courses and advanced training in hopes they could keep working. But no, it was considered their "duty" to go back home, give the jobs to the men. And besides, now women could play with all the enticing household gadgets that were newly available: vacuum cleaners, electric refrigerators, stoves. And by the way, Canada needed new citizens, lots of new citizens.

Still, over the next seven decades, numerous women including me, slowly slipped back into the blue-collar workforce and achieved trade qualifications. By the 1970s, the number of women in skilled blue-collar work in Canada and the US was around 3 percent. As of 2020, fifty years later, that number was about 4 percent in Canada and still 3 percent in the United States.

In the face of a critical skills shortage across the country and the pending retirement of thousands of skilled tradesmen, why has that tiny number barely budged?

Why aren't there more women in trades?

Since the '70s there have been studies, reports, conferences, courses and research galore. The 1985 federal Charter of Rights and Freedoms prohibited discrimination on the basis of gender. There have been, and are, support groups for women in person and on social media. Trades training schools across the country have ongoing commitments to recruiting and training women. There's a #MeToo movement that encourages women to speak up in the face of harassment, summer "hands-on tools" camps for girls, occasional commitments to affirmative action, magazines, newsletters, and role models, including a few tradeswomen who've been promoted to senior positions as forewomen, supervisors and inspectors. And still, the numbers of women have barely budged.

Why aren't there more women in trades?

Recruitment—the number of women *entering* trades—has increased, and when a daring company like Hydro Québec in the 1990s put out an ad specifically inviting women to apply for jobs on its line crews and in other traditionally male work, the response was overwhelming. Something similar happened when the BC government let it be known women and Indigenous peoples would be welcome building the Vancouver Island Highway. At double and triple the rate of standard "women's" wages, who wouldn't be interested?

But most women who enter the trades, don't stay. They last a year, maybe two, then drop out. So, we're doing OK with *recruitment* but failing at *retention*, at keeping women in this work.

Why, then, whenever there's a new grant—federal or provincial—aimed at increasing the number of women in trades, why does the bulk of that money go to research?

I confess, I'm one of those who's been active on the research side. In addition to working on the tools for fifteen years, at the same time I've been writing reports. These include for the BC Human Rights Commission and the BC Institute of Technology, a Master's Thesis, two booklets of interviews of tradeswomen across the country for Labour Canada, a radio program for CBC *Ideas* and a research project with Dr. Marjorie Cohen on women and First Nations on the Vancouver Island Highway, as well as numerous essays and articles in Canadian and international magazines and journals, and many, many speeches and seminars. Also, five books about my personal experience: in addition to this one, a memoir (*Journeywoman*), and three books of poetry.

And I'm only one of several women continuously doing this research since the 1970s. Others include tradeswomen like Marcia Braundy in BC who wrote a published PhD thesis, *Men&Women and Tools,* and Valerie Overend in Saskatchewan.

Yet still, over and over, we hear that whenever an authority has recognized this problem (again) and been given a grant to do something about it (again), a large portion of the money is earmarked (yet again) for research on why there are not more women in trades.

We know why there are not more women in trades!
It's time to talk frankly.

We know the problem is not recruitment but *retention.* The reasons for women dropping out, even when they love the work and are good at it, are primarily two-fold:

1. their isolation as the only, or one of the very few, women on the job, and
2. the culture of the construction workplace with its lack of leadership and responsible management by male foremen and supervisors. As one mechanic told me when I asked why she left the trade, "It wasn't one single thing. It was a whole lot of things." It was the culture.

On isolation:
It's rare for a woman in the trades to work with another woman, let alone with 15 percent women on the crew, the point at which researchers say a group stops being merely token and reaches the status of a minority. It's at that level—15 percent—when being taken seriously happens. Without it, there's never a critical mass, never a sense of solidarity with other women on the site. Being a lone woman on the job is to be considered "odd." Never an invitation to stay.

On the culture, its leadership and management:

You don't have to be a construction worker to know it takes only one bully to poison a workplace, not just for the women but for everyone. And if foremen and supervisors don't immediately discipline that one, the poison festers. Women have enough issues to deal with on a construction site without having to fend off harassment. So they drop out.

When someone is being harassed, everyone on the job knows it. But it's one of the more hurtful and damaging parts of the traditional male culture to put up with it, pretend it's not happening, let the one being harassed deal with it in their own way—and incidentally, hope their rising anxiety levels don't cause them to have an accident.

This is not just an issue of social justice. It's an issue of health and safety, an issue of training enough skilled tradespeople so that we can build and repair and maintain national and provincial infrastructures. And it's not just a gender problem. It's also an issue of every kind of discrimination including racism and homophobia. As one foreman told me, "It doesn't matter if you're purple, as long as you can do the job!"

The point is not to have our infrastructure built by straight white men, it's to have it *built*, period. And even better if the crew get along, and are happy to go to work each morning.

Here's an idea: What if a guy was giving a woman a hard time and instead of laying off the woman, or waiting for her to quit, the foreman fired the harasser? Or even better, what if people on the crew took anti-bullying advice to heart and told the harasser to stop? What if harassers were told, "It doesn't matter what you think. If you want to work here, keep your mouth shut and start acting respectfully. Or you're gone."

Word spreads fast on a construction site. Within a day, everyone would know there was a new standard of behaviour.

We don't need more research on this issue. The problem isn't the women, it's the men, or more precisely, the existing male culture.

It's time for the men who are still a vast majority of the trades to step up, at work, as well as elsewhere. We need the leadership of strong, capable men showing other men how to behave as decent, respectful human beings to *all* employees. We need men courageous enough to risk the discomfort and even ostracization of colleagues in order to create safe, just, productive working environments where women will stay and contribute.

We're in the 21st century now. Macho is out. The new definition of a "strong man" is one who shows strong, fearless leadership.

What are we waiting for?

Most Radical

When I have been on a construction job
six months and
the men count me as a colleague,

when the sun is shining
and the breeze blows
and walls are going up
and we're joking back and forth,

when we've finally accepted
each other as comrades,
carpenters, equals

then it is a miracle,
the impossible made flesh
and this is simply the most radical thing
I have ever done.

—Kate Braid

NOTES

Page 12: I'm grateful to Sheila Norgate (*Storm Clouds Over Party Shoes*) for pointing out, in her own hilarious but poignant way, the evolution of the Nice Girl.

Page 14: Louise Bogan, from the poem, "Women," in *Body of this Death: Poems*. (NY: McBride, 1923).

Page 24: Diane Ackerman, *On Extended Wings*. (NY: Charles Scribner's Sons, 1987), p. 7.

Page 44: Deborah Tannen, *You Just Don't Understand: Women and Men in Conversation* (NY: William Morrow and Company, 1990). In addition to Tannen, see also Robin Lakoff, *Language and Women's Place* (NY: Harper Colophon, 1975) and Dale Spender, *Man Made Language* (Boston: Routledge & Kegan Paul, 1980).

Page 45: Thanks to Stephen Brown, kinesiologist and ergonomist at Simon Fraser University, Burnaby, BC for technical advice and assistance on issues of women's strength. See also *One-Eyed Science: Occupational Health and Women Workers* by Karen Messing (Philadelphia: Temple University Press, 1998).

Page 50: "…damned if you do and damned if you don't…." This was the subject of my Master's Thesis, available as "Invisible Women: Women in Non-Traditional Occupations in B. C.," Department of Communications, Simon Fraser University, 1979.

Page 54: "...totems..." Marie-Josee Legault. Unpublished paper, "Workers' Resistance to Women in Non-Traditional Sectors of Employment and the Role of Unions" (Tele-Université, Montreal, Quebec, 2001). p. 14.

Page 77: Sharon Butala, *The Perfection of the Morning: A Woman's Awakening in Nature.* (Harper Collins, 1994). Also personal communication.

Page 79: Michael Harris, *The End of Absence: Reclaiming What We've Lost in a World of Constant Connection.* (Harper Collins, 2014).

Page 106: Lao Tsu, *Tao Te Ching.* Translation by Gia-Fu Feng and Jane English. (Vintage, NY, 1972).

Page 107: "Courage is the first essential." Katherine Anne Porter. Interview by Barbara Thompson, from *Writers at Work: The Paris Reviw Interviews.* Second Series, ed. by Malcolm Cowley, 1963, *The Paris Review, Inc.* Reprinted by permission of Viking Penguin Inc.

Page 127: Daniel David Moses, Marlin Mosseau and Warren Cariou, as quoted in Sam McKegney, Ed. *Masculindians: Conversations About Indigenous Manhood.* (Winnipeg, MB: University of Manitoba Press, 2014).

Page 129: On women as tokens: Rosabeth Moss Kanter. *Men and Women of the Corporation.* (NY: Basic Books, 1977).

Page 133: The 3 percent figure is taken from research done for my thesis, *Invisible Women: Women in Non-Traditional Occupations in B.C.* (Master of Arts thesis, Simon Fraser University, Department of Communications, 1979.) In the 1970s, neither federal nor provincial governments kept records of women in blue-collar trades, so after phoning large employers around British Columbia, the BC Mining Association and Personnel and Employee Relations departments around the province, etc., the average number of women was around 3 percent. The official numbers since then, and tracked by Statistics Canada across the country, are 5 percent women in blue-collar trades in British Columbia, and 4 percent in Canada as a whole. Thanks to Lisa Langevin, Plumber, Director, Women in Trades, Industry Training Authority, Government of British Columbia for her help on this. Thanks to Susan Eisenberg, Electrician and Resident Scholar, Brandeis University, for information on the US situation. See "Viewpoint: Gender Equity Still is an Industrial Renovation Project," December 18, 2019. The number of 3 percent seems to still roughly hold across the US and the world.

Page 134: Thanks to Anne-Marie Thibault, Mandat, inclusion et diversité, at Hydro Québec for information on their ongoing efforts to encourage women into blue-collar work.

Page 138: Poem, "Most Radical" by Kate Braid. First published in *Turning Left to the Ladies.* (Palimpsest Press, 2009), p. 58.

ACKNOWLEDGEMENTS

Thanks to the following editors and staff of the journals that first published some of these essays, sometimes under slightly different titles:

"…And a Princess." First printed in *Room of One's Own. Vol. 12, Nos. 2&3, "Working for a Living."* Edited by Sandy Shreve, 1989.

"How to Make It Work." Developed for the Trades Discovery for Women program at the British Columbia Institute of Technology (BCIT) in Burnaby, BC, Canada. It was published in a slightly different form in "Training the Excluded for Work: Access and Equity for Women, Immigrants, First Nations, Youth and People with Low Income," ed. Marjorie Griffin Cohen. Vancouver: UBC Press, 2003.

"Making Music." First printed as "The Making of Music: Building Sounds," in *Canadian Women's Studies /Etudes des Femmes.* Winter 1994.

"Constructing Language." First published in The Writers' Union of Canada journal, *Write*, as a Dispatch column. Winter 2018. The more I write, the more I understand how no writer stands alone. I owe deepest thanks to all the women in trades who supported me, who continue to connect with me as we all push in our own ways for change to finally come. You know who you are—thank you! And I thank—again—Tom Wayman who was the first to teach me, mentor me, and who continues to be a stalwart ally in encouraging all of us to write about work and its vital importance in our lives.

I am also deeply grateful to the writing groups who gave invaluable feedback while these pieces were taking shape: the Memoiristas—Heidi Greco, Joy Kogawa, Susan McCaslin, Elsie Neufeld and Marlene Schiwy; and The Muddy Lotus—Zoe Landale, Joy

Thierry Llewellyn, Andrea Spalding and Barbara Stowe. As we all know, no mud, no lotus! (Thanks to Thich Nhat Hahn for that.)

Judy Kujundzic (welder) and Susan Eisenberg (electrician) were generous with technical advice, and it was enormously helpful to speak to Beth Grayer (cabinetmaker) Julie Sawatsky (carpenter) and Tamara Pongracz, Department Head, Trades Access at the BC Institute of Technology, as well as to Anne-Marie Thibault at Hydro Québec in Montréal, for a heads-up on current conditions. Thanks too, to Janet Lane (mechanic) who cheered the whole way.

I'm also deeply grateful to the friends and editors who helped polish the manuscript as it took shape: Janet Alford, Heidi Greco, Vlad Konieczny and Daniel Scott. And Ann West, who happily turned it on its head.

In these days of a critical lack of support for Canadian culture, I can only bow to the good folk at Caitlin Press who labour valiantly to keep Canadian and local poetry and stories alive: Sarah Corsie, Monica Miller and especially editor, publisher and my literary hero, Vici Johnstone. Thank you.